Sacred Shamanic Whispers

Poetic Messages of healing Wisdom

*Healing Journeys Through Ancient
Wisdom, Forgiveness & Love*

A Divine Heretic Book

by
Janine Palmer (Silver Moon) CHT

Sacred Shamanic Whispers

Copyright © 2018 by Janine Palmer (Silver Moon) CHT. All rights reserved.

No part of this publication may be reproduced, stored in a retrieval system or transmitted in any way by any means, electronic, mechanical, photocopy, recording or otherwise without the prior permission of the author except as provided by USA copyright law.

Wolf with ethnic leaves image designed by 0melapics / Freepik.

The opinions expressed by the author are not necessarily those of Stonewall Press.

Published in the United States of America

ISBN: 978-1-948172-56-1 (*sc*)
       978-1-948172-55-4 (*e*)

Library of Congress Control Number: 2018942682

Published by Stonewall Press
4800 Hampden Lane, Suite 200, Bethesda, MD 20814 USA
1.888.334.0980 | www.stonewallpress.com

Poetry
18.08.29

Other books by Janine Palmer

MAIN BOOKS:

Divine Heretic – Standing Holy
Divine Heretic – In Christ Consciousness
Divine Heretic – Sacred Scribe
Divine Heretic – Mystical Fire
Divine Heretic – Alchemist
Divine Heretic – Hierophant
Divine Heretic – Hidden Keys

GENRE SPECIFIC BOOKS
(Material Pulled from Main Books)

Energy Healing Wisdom – Poetic Messages
Spiritual Healing Wisdom – Poetic Messages
Divine Healing Wisdom – Poetic Messages
Rising Above Dogma – Poetic Reflection
For Romance – Poetic Tales & Story Poems
Heart Speak – Poetic Tales & Story Poems
Book of Worthiness – Modern Day Gospel of Good News
Apocalypse of Worthiness – Modern Day Gospel of Good News

This book is dedicated to my family with deep love and to all the people who inspired me to write and to all poets and writers. The poetry contained herein is an acknowledgement to the healing powers of writing. Writing about the importance of processing and releasing emotions becomes artistic expression. Energy needs to flow. These tales are about releasing those blocks. Trust the process of unfolding and spiritual evolvement.

Blessings, love and light.
Janine Palmer (Silver Moon) CHT

Table of Contents

Foreword xv

Sacred Temple

Centuries Standing 2
Castles 3
Purity in Grace 4
Flaming Sword 6
True Face 8
Sacred is Your Lair 10
Aspects of Power 11
Temple Floors 12
Living Doorway 13
Legacy 14
Libraries 16
Of Living Beauty 17
Alchemical Balloon 18

Glimpses of Soul

Friendship 22
Compassion's Lair 24
The Flowering 26
Mystery of My Heart 27
Born of Poetics 28
Vessels 29
Dominant Aspects 30
By Fortune 32
False Assault 33

Mystery & Grace

Divinity's Gate 36
Depths of the Mystery 38
Writings 40

Holy Man 41
Advocate 42
Her Swords 44
Created by You 45
(S)He 47
Mystery's Kiss 49
Disclose the Mystery 50
Haze 52

Mystical & Sacred

A Goddess's Prayer 54
Of My ~ 58
Mystical Order 59
Warrior's Door 60
Sacred Land 62
Cherished 64
Angels 66
Boots and Tunics 68

Divine Wisdom & Energy

Energy Field 70
Focused Energy 71
The Divinity Field 72
Knights of the Order 73
Chainmail 75
Connective 77

Transformative Fire

Torched 80
Twinkle 82
Divine Fire 84
Coals 86
Purification by Fire 87
The Smoke 90
Phoenix Tears 91

Forms of Healing & Forgiveness

On this Journey 94
Tool 97

Truth and Strength and Might 98
Healing Glow 99
Prescriptions 100
Stillness 101
Guided 102
Mirror of Forgiveness 104
Their Return 106
Fountain of Forgiveness 107
The Emotion 109
Seemingly Unforgiveable 110
Meditation 112

Ascension & Spiritual Alchemy

Thistle and Weeds 116
Her Queen's Speech 118
Tribes 119
Aspects 121
Sovereign 122
Emotions as Teachers 123
Waves of Love 124
Rebirth 125

Your Magnificence & Worthiness

Sweet Soul 128
Vicinity 130
Separation Snare 131
Reverent 132
Sins Against Self 133
Broken Angel 135
The Compliment of Truth 138
Holy Fire 139
Forgetful 140
Come Closer 141
Your Beauty 142

Blessed Be Our Magic

Magical Branches and Roots 144
Her Magic 146

Cauldron Brew 148
Mistress of Magic 149
The Priestess 151
Cathedral of the Forest 152

Your Own Honor

Her Armor 156
Your Truth Again 158
Quill 159
Inner Planes 160
Quiet Defiance 161
Healing Flame 162
Quiet Wisdom 164
Our Sacred Lands 165

Mirror, Mirror

Mighty 168
Mirror of the Vagabond 170
Our Own Spark 171
God's Creatures 172
Observe 173
Down Times 174
Beauty of the Creator in All 175
Boomerang Words & Deeds 177

Shedding Skins & Shells

No Rights to Slavery 180
The Burden 183
Beckoning Intent 184
Destruction 186
The Path 188
The Love 190
Tangled Threads 191
False Hell 193
Countless Pieces 194
Born from the Wreckage 195
Proud and Lonely 196
Shedding Skins 197

Initiations & Battle Scars

Experiences as Tools 200
War or Peace.. 201
Blood Stains...202
Not My Business..204
The Plow 206
Unknown/Unseen...207
Dastardly Deeds 209
Echoes.. 210
Cave of Initiation 211
Inner Battles.. 213
The Hard Parts 214
Enemies Rising (?) 215

Judgment & Ego

Guidelines... 218
The Lower..220
Release 222
Negativity 223
Self-Discovery or Ego? 225
Unrecognized Angels... 227
Wounded Light...228
Perception's Roots..230
Screaming Ego.. 231

The Suffering & Shadow

Karmic Challenges 234
Less Elegant... 235
The Shadow Side..236
Corrections & Alignments 239
Disgraceful 240
Lessons 241
Wicked..243
Wounded Healers 245
Twisted 246
By Degrees 247
The Healed 248
Unaware...249

Shadows of Ghosts...250
Hell Bent...251
The Dark..252

Illusion and the Veil

Make Believe..256
Twice Born..257
Destructive Entanglements...259
Priests of Unity..260
Illusion's Wings...262
Process of Empowerment..263
Illusion's Loom..264
The Power of Voice...265
The Mystery of the Heart 267
Evil Does Not Rule It..269

Beyond Masks & Disguise

Honey or Venom 272
Dark Night...273
War Lords...275
Mighty Castle from the Stones..277
Of Many Names Yet Nameless 279
Declaration...280
Attack of Trust 282
Unless & Until...283

Light Through the Cracks

The Path to Light 286
Columns of Light 287
Encourage...289
Sunlight and Shadow...290
Graves 291
Wounded..292
The Broken Ones 294
Crack You Open 295
Investments...296
Not Remembered..297
By Responsibility Untold...298

Freedom Through Awakening

Collective 300
Collars 302
Healed Ancestors 303
Oh, Karma 305
Waves 306
Divine Solutions 307

Into Knowing, Beyond Belief

It's Called Wild Road 310
Honor the Spirits 312
Sacred Power 313
In the (K)now 314
Moving Beyond 316

Metaphors & Deeper Truth

Agents of the Gods 318
Weak Links 320
Appear to Face 321
Not Intentional 322
Darkness's Host 324
Temperate 326
Witches' Wings 328
Created and/or Creative 330
Blood Soaked Virgin 331
The Gods 333
Of 1000 Names Yet Nameless 334
Channel 335

Perspectives & Treasures

The Secrets 338
Doors 340
Transition to Treasure 341
Home 343
Teacher and Student 344
Shock Therapy 346
Hostages 347
Tidal 349

Rejection 350
Limited Perspective 351
New Doors 352
Falling Out 354
The Colors of Love 355
Lay Down Your Arms 357
Depth Perception 359
Building Philosophies 360
The Lion's Map 362
You Become What You Hunt 363
The Leather Pouch 364

Stories, Guides & Whispers of Love

Kingdom of Compassion & the Company of Horses 368
The Dragon's Seeds 370
Sleeping Dragon 372
Mermaid Song 374
Say Yes 376
A Scabbard with No Sword 378
Spinning 379
Airborne 381
It Was the Dragon 383
Satchel 385
Seeds of Intention 386
Found 388
Halo 391
About the Author 393

Foreword

Along my ongoing awakening and healing journey, I've learned many ancient healing modalities for emotional and spiritual healing. Messages for shedding skins and shells and rising out of the ashes are shared in the poetic messages in this book. After becoming certified in Reiki and Hypnotherapy, I became certified as a Shamanic practitioner. Over the period of about three years, I wrote eight books of poetic healing messages. This book contains many which tie in with shamanic training and practices for healing on many levels and releasing what no longer serves.

Shamanic Healing work involves and includes journey work, meditative journeys where we meet guides to help us heal any manner of issues. Some of the poetic messages shared here will be like taking short journeys when you read them. Certain ones resonate more deeply with different people. Often they make one go deeply into areas where work is needed, where things need to be acknowledged, thanked, forgiven and released. They offer ideas for working through issues. They offer tools.

Everyone is on their own healing journey. The messages here are to promote deeper thinking; to remind us of the importance of forgiveness for true freedom, to release guilt, shame, resentment, grief, anger, fear, sadness and unforgiveness, in order to clear energetic blocks so energy can flow freely for our well-being on many levels. Each experience and response is unique. This is a reminder of your magnificence and your worthiness and to remember to love yourself.

Janine Palmer (Silver Moon) CHT

Sacred Temple

Centuries Standing

Gazing up at the majesty,
Of a standing stately one,
Anchoring heaven and earth in beauty,
In this realm as it is done.

The branches which anchor it to heaven,
The roots which anchor it to the earth,
The keepers of ancient knowledge,
Assisting man through his rebirth.

Assisting in shelter and beauty,
Providing food for body and food for thought.
If one takes the time to wonder and ponder,
The pieces of Mystery through illusions not caught.

In strength through centuries standing,
And if you ask them they will speak,
They will share ancient mysteries and guidance,
To those open and brave enough to seek.

What a comfort to take in their beauty,
The music whispering through their leaves,
And the stories they could tell you of history,
Which they have stood in grace to see.

The vibration of their sacred energy,
Exists in so many things,
The beauty of grain and fragrance,
Makes some hearts in gratitude sing.

Inspired by the beautiful old oak trees in Ickworth Park, England

Janine Palmer (Silver Moon)

Castles

Castles were part of her lineage,
In other realities parallel and before,
Places of residence or given away,
Through light and shadow's doors.

Her heart is a sacred castle,
Where treasures are stored so deep,
From whence came her love and compassion,
Through the sacred door of her temple keep.

But in that space she carried sadness,
The wounds from battles long fought,
She was called to help others through their trials,
But there are prices for things which are sought.

Experiencing battles with loved ones,
Parts of the heart are harmed time and again,
Being harmed by them leaves the deepest scars,
Which are often mistaken to be sin.

Weight upon weight, the burdens,
Which become too heavy after time,
They are the deadened leaves,
Which we must trim away from the vine.

Everything serves a purpose,
And the seeker will begin to see,
What is learned and compromised,
What binds us or sets us free.

Janine Palmer (Silver Moon)

Purity in Grace

They misunderstood the word virgin,
Due to mistranslation so misleading,
The original word in the original language,
Simply meant a young woman without any sexual meaning.

And also what they misunderstand,
About some being upon earth here from God,
Is that the virgin refers to the pureness of spirit,
The pureness of heart and soul, upon which so many trod.

The inviolable pureness of spirit,
Impenetrable from forces of dark,
And that is the vessel so chosen.
To usher in the chosen ones of pure heart.

It has nothing to do with physical acts,
Man has been brainwashed for far too long,
No matter the experience with soul mates on earth,
They do not affect the purity of her heart's song.

She is a pure servant of God,
No matter who she is called to love here,
No matter who is chosen to nurture her soul,
To the masses through illusion this is so unclear.

Some intuitive people can sense this,
The pureness of a heart and soul,
Those who are here doing work for the collective,
Even though others throw stones.

Their stones can't touch the purity,
Their venomous words also cannot,
Their false beliefs and opinions,
Create foulness on earth which rots.

If you sense such purity,
In any being upon your path,
Befriend the goodness of God in them,
And lay down your useless gaff.

The physical body isn't as pure as the spirit,
It's a temporary suit of clothes,
The spirit now is eternal,
A curious mixture in how it glows.

Janine Palmer (Silver Moon)

Flaming Sword

It was time for her to rise from the depths,
When she came up from the depths of the black,
She came out clothed in her full power of light,
With a flaming sword to restore their power back.

The Feminine had lost her power,
Ignorance had taken it away,
While they continued the debilitating cycles,
And they knew not to whom they prayed.

So beguiled by illusions still dancing,
Limited understanding and limited perspectives ruled,
They trudged along in their supreme ignorance,
Not even knowing they had been fooled.

Such a limited idea of God,
Do most earthly beings carry around,
Not in touch with the truth of their own spirit,
Their own truth still waiting to be found.

So many sheep being led around,
By bridles of illusion controlled by fear,
And so they continue to harm each other,
While a form of constricting darkness, is feeding off their tears.

She transformed after spending time in darkness,
Because in the darkness is where she would rise,
From the illusions which had controlled her,
Where she would break free in solitude from the guise.

This type of darkness had served her,
This type of darkness was a womb,
Where transformation and rebirth were created,
From a place which a first felt like a tomb.

She found parts of herself waiting there,
And it was there she found her sword,
The sword of her infinite power,
Her inner kingdom, her truth, her hoard.

The treasures within unbeknownst to her,
Until she was thrust into the dark and the deep,
Only to discover there were gifts in disguise,
Things waiting and protected in her temple keep.

Her flaming sword she now carried,
And certain beings could see its light,
They found support and compassion in her,
And from it they strengthened their might.

Her sword was fueled by compassion,
Her sword was a beacon of light,
Her sword was perpetual love burning,
Guiding them in from the night.

She was here to do work for the collective,
She was here to do work for God from love,
She carried with her an awareness of the attributes,
Of the balance between the raven and the dove.

From the dark comes magnificent creation,
The dark is a type of womb,
From the dark we can experience healing,
As we are woven upon the cosmic loom.

Light is a healing energy,
Light serves our journey too,
Nothing is ever one sided,
You will know this when we remember what you knew.

Janine Palmer (Silver Moon)

True Face

Beneath her cloak was freedom,
Which not everyone could see,
She had to lose what she thought she wanted,
In order to be free.

The order of the mystery,
The order of learning in grace,
The order of the illusion,
Behind the disguise is our true face.

The cloak hid treasures and mysteries,
The cloak was protection as well,
The cloak was a type of illusion,
While we live in this temporary spell.

She discovered something very important,
That she could count on no one but herself,
Due to misinterpretation and misunderstanding,
We create many different kinds of hell.

It is only when we detach from expectations,
When notions of fairy tales take their leave,
That we find freedom and truth in rising above,
The illusions to which we cleave.

The abstract visions ever changing,
Stories are created and destroyed,
And happiness is found in wanting nothing,
When grace has been deployed.

She experienced love and was grateful,
But it was part of the illusion here,
Any love experienced in another,
Exists in ourselves, beyond our fears.

The true face of our being,
Can be glimpsed in our sacred heart,
When we can give, expecting nothing,
Because from love we are never apart.

The love you feel for someone,
Is something which never goes away,
It's our ideas attached to wanting,
Creating illusions which must be slayed.

She came to a place of acceptance,
Of letting go after the lessons of loss,
Cutting cords like shackles so binding,
To rise above the dross.

By freeing herself from their limitations,
She found parts of herself unknown,
Then truer friends came along her path,
As new blessings were being shown.

The key was to have no attachment,
The key was to let things flow free,
The key was to find happiness in the moment,
Free of the past or the future unseen.

The future is ever unfolding,
Which you create here with your thoughts unending,
And you learn by so much experience,
Like branches of a great tree ever bending.

Janine Palmer (Silver Moon)

Sacred is Your Lair

Even though I am trusting,
I have had to beware of trust,
Because people I have loved and trusted,
Turned the hinges on my heart to rust.

People here we think we know,
Because our stories we have shared,
Now have ammunition to use against us,
Because our heart and soul we bared.

Underhanded ignorance,
Intermingled with crafty lies,
So they can spit their venom at us,
After removing their disguise.

Beware the masks will quickly fall,
When thou least expects,
They might try to make your life a shambles,
Because their energy is a wreck.

These violent acts and behaviors,
Come from their wounds unhealed,
They will test you up on your path,
But your sacred power you should not yield.

We might be able to help someone heal,
But we are not a board at which to throw darts,
We must command the respect we deserve.
To honor the grace of our hearts.

Protect yourself on your journey,
If you're going to share your love be aware,
Be aware that things will come and go,
And sacred is your lair.

Janine Palmer (Silver Moon)

Aspects of Power

The power of who you've been before,
Exists deep within you now;
Along this path you might find pieces of it,
As all the challenges show you how.

The lessons from so long ago,
If time was a linear thing,
Are ingrained in your spiritual DNA,
For the wisdom they will bring.

But somehow we must awaken,
To the parts and to the power,
All stored away for safest keeping,
In our spiritual temple tower.

This body serves our purpose here,
As we endeavor to awake,
For our service and enlightenment,
For the benefit of the collective's sake.

Who you were before,
Once upon a time,
Is stored in the complexity of you now,
All still connected to the vine.

Janine Palmer (Silver Moon)

Temple Floors

Reach deep for that pain you've buried,
The pain that's trying to come out,
That negative energy toxic to your being,
The reason we cry and shout.

But we don't only cry and shout,
Sometimes we treat others in the cruelest ways,
And that is not the vibration we should stay in,
Say the Ancient of Days.

We experience things to learn from,
But nastiness we should not to carry,
Take the wisdom then rise above,
You're not a tomb for things to be buried.

You are a temple which needs maintaining,
Sweep clean your temple floors,
Open the windows to let in the light,
Feel the breeze when you open the doors.

Let in the winds of spirit,
To sweep in and clear away the old,
Breathe it in deeply for cleansing,
The depths of your glorious soul.

Clear the clutter off the shelves,
Stored inside you somewhere,
To restore that twinkle to your eyes,
To replace that burdensome glare.

Crack a smile in beauty,
As you break out of any old shells,
Shed old skins, refreshed and renewed,
Because within you sacred divinity dwells.

Janine Palmer (Silver Moon)

Living Doorway

We are a living doorway,
Connected always to the divine,
And the love and purity of grace,
Is ever yours and mine.

An ember burns within us,
A brilliant sacred spark,
Our own inner candle flame,
To light our way through the dark.

The kingdom within our majesty,
Something forgotten when we ventured here,
But it is always accessible within us,
When we open our ears to hear.

When we listen to the whispers,
Of the divinity of our heart and soul,
Which speaks to us from our inner kingdom,
So kindled by our glow.

The doorway is higher connection,
The spirit descended into matter,
And it speaks so quietly to us,
Above and beyond our ego mind chatter.

Our doorway to divinity,
Is a sacred part of our self,
Waiting to be rediscovered,
When we tap into our well.

Janine Palmer (Silver Moon)

Legacy

What legacy do you come from?
What legacy shall you leave?
Will you help your brethren heal?
Or will you cause any of them to grieve?

Are you controlled by the rod?
Or do you contribute to its power?
Do you help the collective thrive on the vine?
Are you helping it now to flower?

Some people stand on their own piles of shite,
Creating more obstacles for us to work around,
As we try to clean up so much debris,
For needed balance to be found.

We need to clean up our messes,
We need to contribute in some helpful way,
We need to stand in power against harmful negativity,
Our own demons we need to slay.

And to slay the remnants of falsehoods,
Which they fed us when we were young,
Through fears and insecurities,
Of incomplete dogma which has stung.

The veil over our eyes and ears,
Out of fear our truth we block,
Due to a force against us,
Which doesn't want us to find the key to our locks.

We won't find the keys through man-made religions,
Although some of them point the way,
Others are tools of negative darkness,
And in confusion they want us to stay.

When we find our very own truth,
The legacy within ourselves,
The confusion magically vanishes,
And no longer are we in hell.

When we find our inner power,
When we rise above our own ash,
That's when we reunite with God within us,
And no longer do we identify with lack.

The legacy of the truth of your temple,
The glorious kingdom within,
To be found when we all rise above,
The erroneous notion of sin.

Janine Palmer (Spirit Silver Moon)

Libraries

The libraries of creation,
So safely stored away,
Not discovered 'til one is ready,
To walk the truth, the light and the way.

The libraries contain our history,
Of so many experiences before,
The spiritual and the physical,
Through so many forgotten doors.

Parts of it are disconnected,
Until we do the work to reconnect,
Which we do or don't do by free will,
As our choices and learning redirect.

Pieces of the Mystery,
Then and now and still unformed,
Flickering faintly through the veil,
Seen when masks are no longer worn.

To shred the skins and shells,
To uncover truth so much more deep,
To the treasure chest which lies within,
Our sacred castle keep.

We are libraries of information,
We are unaware, walking in sleep,
Of the depth of wisdom, of creation,
Then and now in grace so deep.

The kingdom within, our library,
Created from Love far beyond,
And when we begin to awaken,
Our hearts and souls respond.

Janine Palmer (Silver Moon)

Of Living Beauty

The living beauty of the spirit,
Eternal and brilliant and free,
Glistens and glitters in magnificence,
As it flickers in and out of thee.

Beneath the earthly clothes you wear,
The physical armor which houses your soul,
To learn through experiences good or bad,
Life like a river it ebbs and flows.

Do you flow around obstacles?
Do you disrespect others due to belief?
Do you walk with the glow of divine love?
Or is darkness a familiar thief?

The living beauty is within you,
And it is also in your brother,
We are all connected to the sacred vine,
But our magnificence has been smothered.

Smothered by misinterpretation,
Smothered by dogma's dark box,
Smothered by illusions and fears running rampant,
But who holds the keys to our locks?

It is we who hold the sacred keys,
The keys to our truth behind the chatter,
The keys to the love and light of our soul,
The living beauty which descended into matter.

The living beauty is our compassion,
The living beauty is our own Grace,
The living beauty is ever present forgiveness,
And we are our very own gate.

Janine Palmer (Silver Moon)

Alchemical Balloon

She went to her energetic garden for healing,
To her sacred, meditative place,
Where she could interact with her angels and guides,
In higher realms which work through grace.

She wanted to let go of old woundedness,
From sources which to her were unknown,
She wanted to release programs and triggers,
To allow guidance and wisdom to be shown.

In her garden she was met by Merlin,
Such a wise and wonderful sage,
A supportive force of ancient wisdom,
With her for more than an age.

He guided her to pull out any energy,
From any life experience before,
Anything which triggered old wounds,
To remove it then and there forevermore.

He placed a copper bowl before her,
To place the discarded energy into that,
Then he grinned a knowing grin,
And tipped his wizard's hat.

She pulled out any energy of judgment,
Of her own or from anyone else,
She pulled out any lingering doubt,
Unlocking doors to any cells.

As she placed the energy into the bowl,
In a big swirling energetic ball,
She was sweeping her temple floors,
To be of better service to the All.

She pulled out any pain from misunderstanding,
Of anything from misperception's lens,
And lighter her being became,
Through this energetic cleanse.

She pulled out any sadness,
Which once affected her heart,
She pulled out any random weapons,
Like knives or arrows or darts.

She pulled out the limiting effects of illusion,
She pulled out caring what others think,
She pulled out any resentment or unforgiveness,
Only from love would she drink.

She pulled out any feelings of unworthiness,
Even from others which was not her own,
She pulled out any feelings of obligation,
Or feeling that for anyone else she must atone.

She knew we balance karma through love,
And by forgiving ourselves first and foremost,
And that we must not dwell in lower vibrational energies,
Which can become darkness's diabolical host.

The ball of debilitating energies was large,
Which Merlin transformed into a big balloon with a string,
She sent it up through violet flame on to Source, escorted by angels,
And with gratitude her soul now did sing.

He said her being was happier,
To be free of those energies at last,
He had her put her hands upon her heart,
And breathe in deep to anchor it fast.

He had her draw in healing energy,
From the highest source,
To fill the emptied places with love,
For the next part of her journey's course.

Janine Palmer (Silver Moon/Owl Feather)

Glimpses of Soul

Friendship

She said, I've misunderstood what friendship is,
I must have misunderstood what it should be;
Or maybe I misunderstood that it's not meant to last,
Or at least not like I thought that it would, you see.

I suppose we don't realize how people change,
How they evolve and grow or not,
I suppose we are very unaware,
Of the burdens they carry which rot.

I suppose that lack of communication,
And lack of compassion are key,
To why doors get locked and can't be opened,
And friendships slip away from you and me.

It seems we forgot how to treat one another,
It seems like such a loss,
But these things redirect us to other better things,
And a trade-off is the cost.

But what we take away from it,
Is always our gift to keep,
And if they mistreat us for reasons unknown,
We must move on after we weep.

Sometimes we don't have enough defined boundaries,
Because we are in a space of misplaced trust,
We trusted that being to be there for us,
But on the hinges of their heart was unseen rust.

We mistakenly thought we could be ourselves,
That we would be accepted fully as we are,
But what we seem to fail to realize,
Is that can't happen due to their scars.

Their scars or ours can create barriers,
Things needing healing will eventually come out,
And the face of the wounds when the masks falls off,
Is what our learning experiences are all about.

To recognize the wound in another,
Or to recognize the wound in ourselves,
Is the key to taking a step back from taking it personally,
So we are not drawn into that hell.

New friends will always be sent to us,
New blessings to replace what we miss,
We must not stay too attached to anything,
Or we will steal away our own bliss.

Here's to the friends who have loved us,
Here's to the friends we have lost,
Here's to the new friends we haven't yet met,
And here's to the blessings not affected by loss.

Janine Palmer (Silver Moon)

Compassion's Lair

Sounds reverberate through the air,
Through ears and minds and hearts so fair,
Inspiration from the words of friends,
To write from the heart, a message to send.

To share sweet love from compassion's lair,
To disconnect from illusion's snare,
Ups and downs and dark and light,
When there is balance, we find our might.

As everyone fights a challenging battle,
And sometimes we find our cages do rattle,
What others battle is often unknown,
Unless and until they let it be shown.

Sometimes when we endeavor to share in trust,
And through the hinges break the rust,
Only to find it to be used against,
Against us in the cruelest sense.

All for the learning some would say,
Because this shows us our powers along the way,
How will we rise or how will we fall?
Should we or shouldn't we communicate at all?

Because lack of communication can so disrupt,
Connections can cease to function so abrupt,
Misunderstandings due to lack of facts,
And people not knowing how to proceed or act.

Things felt but not spoken, then remain unknown,
And love is not shared, because love was not shown,
What once was alive, withers on the vine,
Actions or lack of action, interpreted as unkind.

Fear which stops with armor in place,
Fear of loss which seems stronger than grace,
Old habits and patterns disrupt our course,
The obstacles which throw us from the horse.

Until we find inside us, something hidden all this time,
We find a warrior's strength, which is always yours and mine,
Deciding to lay down our burdens, for our being to be light,
To die to the old after the experience, of our soul's dark night.

Compassion must be present, to gain our greatest strength,
And if we don't discover it, we will suffer at great length,
Compassion is a crucial key, a gift of power from on high,
When shared with ourselves and others, our wings again can fly.

Janine Palmer (Silver Moon)

The Flowering

The flowering of her soul on earth,
For a purpose she couldn't explain,
And some of them would try to shut her down,
But for it nothing would they gain.

Her flowering some would witness,
Her flowering some would ignore,
Her flowering some might be jealous of,
As she walked through mysterious doors.

Some would endeavor to support her,
Some would test her in painful ways,
Some would set traps to trip her up,
As they trudged along through earth's dark maze.

But when her inner strength would guide her,
Along with the words of the angels who spoke,
Were beings who guided her onward,
Who helped her with her yoke.

The ones who tried to knock her down,
Would become the stepping stones to help her climb,
And they would unknowingly inspire her,
To help others through experience and rhyme.

Janine Palmer (Silver Moon)

Mystery of My heart

Not many know the Mystery,
Which resides here hidden in me,
But it is a powerful, beautiful force,
When it flows nurtured, bold and free.

Sometimes it's elastic,
Sometimes it's glowing light,
Sometimes it's pure compassion,
Sometimes it's closed up tight.

Sometimes is holds such sadness,
Which always needs to be released,
Because illusion is a liar,
And fear can be a thief.

Angels often fly with me,
They remind me to release,
To let go of what doesn't serve me,
To never carry guilt, or shame, or grief.

All these emotions must be processed,
And in the end forgiveness must reign,
Because my heart is an amazing conductor of love,
No one who knows it will leave the same.

My love here is God's love,
Love that touches grace at levels deep,
My heart is a valiant castle,
My heart is a mysterious keep.

My heart is a mystery to many,
But there are some who see right through,
To the truth of who I really am,
Someone familiar they always knew.

Janine Palmer (Silver Moon)

Born of Poetics

Created from places way down deep,
Flowing from places which quietly weep,
A depth of love for which there are no words,
Desperately wanting now to be heard.

Trails of mystery, partially exposed,
And you can almost smell the scent of the rose,
Heartstrings played in individual tunes,
Fortunes told and shared like runes.

Ancient mystery seeping out,
Through whisper, thought or painful shout,
Feelings expressed from passions born,
Or heart wrenching pain from love so torn.

Navigating through illusions as we weave,
Sifting through the truths and falsehoods to which we cleave,
Sharing our love or sharing our fears,
While learning to heal what caused our tears.

Born of poetics, communication displayed,
And the beauty produced, we would not trade,
Fancy and fantasy with experience combined,
And the stories shared are yours and mine.

Janine Palmer (Silver Moon)

Vessels

What a mystery are our bodies,
Vessels here for our evolution,
Vessels with hidden treasures and wisdom,
We are our own solution.

But first we must navigate the curious mists,
The illusions and the veil,
Our vessel is our temple,
And to nothing should it be nailed.

We might empty it sometimes,
Sharing so much of ourselves,
And it must be refilled with love,
Our vessels are where love dwells.

Give and take in balance,
So we give shall we receive,
As we find our truth and knowing,
Above and beyond belief.

Things are rarely what they seem,
And beliefs might point the way,
Rigidity causes branches to snap,
The healthy ones know how to sway.

Our vessel is a holy thing,
To serve a purpose here,
A sacred house for our spirit and soul,
As we rise out of falsehoods and fear.

Our vessels carry the greatest love,
Which is always meant to be shared,
And the greatest blessings come back to us,
When through grace we show we care.

Janine Palmer (Silver Moon)

Dominant Aspects

There are dominant aspects of our being,
Which to others will stand out,
Whether serious, shy or humorous,
They might reflect what our journey is about.

Some of us are very old souls,
We have descended here many times,
We might seem out of place here,
While we are working with the vine.

So serious is our nature,
As we have important work to do,
But we still make time for laugher,
As our angels tell us to.

Tending to the many,
In thought, or word, or deed,
Messengers sent to help them heal,
To staunch the wounds which bleed.

There are those who bring us humor,
They bring needed smiles to our face,
It comes from their comforting presence,
Sent as they were from Grace.

Some are humorous beings,
Because it's so important that we laugh,
That we overcome the ignorance of darkness,
When we remove its unseen gaff.

Sometimes disguised as light,
Darkness is a clever lord,
It makes us believe things which are not true,
And calls it God's own word.

God's word is ever within you,
They once heard Jesus say,
The kingdom of God is within you,
But outside of ourselves we are swayed.

Some of them are quiet,
Some who observe to learn might seem shy,
They are simply seekers here,
As are you and I.

Janine Palmer (Silver Moon)

By Fortune

By fortune do we journey,
By what was written by us upon divine scrolls,
And by our free will choice and agency,
Cause-and-effect and consequence as Destiny rolls.

Things we agreed to experience here,
Through people and situations good or bad,
And how we react is our own choice,
Whether we feel happy or sad.

Different perspectives are always present,
If we are open enough to see,
If we realize we are always learning,
And move out too much attachment to be free.

By fortune we give and receive love,
By fortune we learn not to blame,
By fortune we learn the beauty of forgiveness,
So we can avoid being hobbled and lame.

By fortune we rise above ego,
Ego which serves us but should not be our master,
Because when we do crash and burn,
We rise out of the ashes much faster.

By fortune we hold nothing against our brother,
By fortune we hold nothing against ourselves,
By fortune we become our own healer,
As treasures and tools throughout life are shown.

Janine Palmer (Silver Moon)

False Assault

I have learned to feel through emotions,
And in earnest do I strive,
To move beyond the experience,
With new wisdom do I thrive.

How I react to anything,
No matter how it appears,
Might include the release of pain,
Through the river of my tears.

Even though I may not understand,
Why someone would treat me so cruel,
I must consider their unhealed wounds,
And not let it shackle me like a fool.

I'm in full charge and power,
If how I do or don't react,
And I have found in not reacting,
I take my power back.

When I react to their negativity,
I give my power to them by default,
And that is not the best way now,
To be drawn in by false assault.

I am always learning something,
About others and myself,
And a wonderful treasure I have unearthed,
Is that I am the key to any cell.

Janine Palmer (Silver Moon)

Mystery & Grace

Divinity's Gate

In between the mystery,
Are doorways we might take,
For exiting the ignorance zone,
On the path of wisdom for our sake.

An exercise in removing the shackles,
In which so much of mankind is bound,
For enlightenment and higher wisdom,
Through our inner truth it's found.

Breaking free from control systems,
So called organized groups which sell,
Partial truths mixed with falsehoods,
And they use your fear of brimstone and hell.

Programming people with all types of fear,
While passing the collection plate,
Selling something which is ever free,
While perpetrating hate.

Not all of them are like that,
Thank the gods for favors small,
And for sending brave beings to help heal humanity,
For the greater good of the all.

There are so many things to learn,
Of your free will and own accord,
To free yourself from earthly illusions,
And the useless fears you've stored.

To find beauty, so much truth and beauty,
Waiting in your kingdom within,
Put there by your Creator,
Discovered when your journey begins.

Compassion ever flowing there,
Intuitive knowing of sacred wisdom,
Remember your magnificence now,
And forgiveness is always part of the vision.

The keys of sacred truth,
We realize we possess when we awake,
Not part of any particular group,
Connected with God through divinity's gate.

Janine Palmer (Silver Moon)

Depths of the Mystery

As we discover the depths of the Mystery,
One experience at a time,
We rise above the preoccupation and falsehood,
Of the idea of yours and mine.

The more we learn, the more we realize,
The less we really know,
We hunger for more knowledge or remembering,
Ancient and sacred wisdom then and now bestowed.

The more we learn and rediscover,
The wiser in some ways we feel,
But there is so much more for us to learn,
And we learn more when we heal.

Unhealed wound of emotions,
Are debilitating stumbling blocks,
We must attend as well to the spirit,
Which can guide us to the locks.

The mind is a curious, challenging thing,
Which should never be in charge of the heart,
This disconnected state of duality,
Creates separation and keeps us apart.

Be aware that the separation,
Between the higher and lower selves,
And the debilitating way we perceive our brethren,
Is a backwards kind of hell.

The Mystery is the descent here,
Where spirit doth mingle with matter,
Where we are challenged with illusions,
And the incessant ego mind chatter.

The programming and conditioning,
With falsehoods and with fear,
Deeper into and away from the Mystery,
To discover or not, my dear.

The Mystery extends to the depth of you,
To answers and knowledge within,
To sacred wisdom hidden there,
The kingdom in the silence beyond the din.

Janine Palmer (Silver Moon)

Writings

Writings upon papyrus,
Writings on paper or on bark,
Writings upon ancient codices,
For what knowledge they might spark.

The wisdom for the initiate,
Which he or she might take away,
When it sparks the truth of his or her inner knowledge,
Of the truth, the light and the way.

To discover the depths of the Mystery,
To gain pearls of wisdom here,
The reason for our descent,
Into this place of love and fear.

Take from the writings what you will,
But know that they are not God,
They are only pinpoints of light,
Which point you to the rod.

Janine Palmer (Silver Moon)

holy Man

A holy man can be many things,
Many things programmed people might not expect,
God can work though him in disguise,
Which the masses in their error reject.

A holy man is a seeker,
Discovering the depths of the Mystery,
A holy man is one who honors his brethren,
Having risen above dogma and now is free.

A holy man might not seem to conform,
To any limited understanding of right or wrong,
But following the God given wisdom of his soul,
He will answer to his own understanding of divinity's song.

He will likely not be trapped by interpretation of scriptures,
Because far above and beyond such things,
The trail of light he will leave in this world,
Will cause many a man and woman to sing.

He will not try to control others,
Because his ego is not in charge of him now,
He will see the beauty through the masks,
His inner light has shown him how.

His holiness is God shining through,
It is as purely simple as that,
Even though he sits not on a church pew in judgement,
And he doesn't wear self-righteousness as a hat.

When people break free from their ideas,
From their need to ever be right,
When they rise above their egos in awakening,
Is when they see the light.

Janine Palmer (Silver Moon)

Advocate

She was an advocate for so many,
For many people and many things,
She answered the call of her heart and soul,
For the challenges that would bring.

She was a voice for those who suffer,
She helped in as many ways as could be,
Honoring many people along her path,
Because there are so many ways we're not free.

She found she had to be careful,
Experiences made her more aware,
That people would try to take advantage of her kindness,
So there had to be boundaries there.

People would be drawn to her for help,
And she would do what she could for each,
But there were those along the way who mistreated her,
These are the things this life will teach.

The mistreatment came from fears,
The mistreatment came from pain,
The mistreatment came from jealousy,
It came from anger with nothing to gain,

What they would end up doing,
Would be to push her well away,
But often when people come across her path,
They're not really meant to stay.

So many times people don't intend it,
They don't intend harm in any way,
It's just their pain and insecurities,
Which create obstacles day by day.

It's important not to hold it against them,
If we can help it in any way at all,
Because if we do, we give our power away,
And loss of power can make us fall.

She will always be an advocate,
But her boundaries must be in place,
She must protect herself for her journey,
So she can function through her grace.

Janine Palmer (Silver Moon)

her Swords

He'd heard about the woman,
The one with the power of the sword,
But not only the ancient power therein contained,
There was the power of the Word.

The sword she placed within the stone,
And then she picked up the pen,
As mighty or mightier than Excalibur,
For the wisdom it brought in.

The knowledge for the learning,
The messages of hope so rare,
For them to heal their hearts and souls,
Because of their beauty within so fair.

The pen to kindle the fires,
The fire within the soul,
The ink weaving in intricate pieces of the Mystery,
From the Angels here all aglow.

Messages from divinity,
For those who care to read,
And the wisdom becomes their freedom,
From ignorance, hate and greed.

The pen across the parchment,
Dancing in creative symphony divine,
To give them glimpses of truth and beauty,
Which connects them to the vine.

Words of love and wisdom,
Straight from the Mystery,
To enter their hearts and souls and minds,
So in their power they can stand free.

Janine Palmer (Silver Moon)

Created by You

Co-creator's with God we are,
Masculine and Feminine combined,
In an earthly body for initiations,
In the illusion of space and time.

Will you create here?
For yourself or for another?
What legacy will you leave here,
For your children and your brothers?

This free will zone of creation,
Where the Angels don't interfere,
Unless and until we ask them,
We must invite them in my dear.

We have unseen help all around us,
We have so many helpful tools,
But due to the veil and illusion,
Most stumble around like fools.

So engrossed in the physical world,
So thirsty for material things,
It's only when the spirit awakens,
That we begin to discover the treasures the Mystery brings.

What you experience around you,
Was in some way created by you,
Perhaps you drew it in,
For lessons to come through.

The people you accept into your life,
Will be challenging or gifts you will see,
They will benefit you or test you,
To become who you need to be.

How you allow them to treat you,
And how you choose to react,
Will lead you down a merry trail,
Either to abundance or to lack.

Be very careful and aware,
Of what do you to create,
Because that is part of the road you walk,
What will be the next gate?

Janine Palmer (Silver Moon)

(S)he

One and the same now separate,
But they are one and the same now still,
In higher realms or lower,
In how they love and feel.

There is no separation, really,
It's illusion which so grossly rapes,
No superiority over parts of the whole,
Unless viewed from hellish gates.

(S)He is the Creator,
(S)He is you and me,
(S)He is the ever present truth and reality,
Which the sleeping cannot see.

(S)He is the highest Love,
To separate is to fall,
To linger in self-righteous superiority,
Is to disconnect from the All.

(S)He is you and I,
In our original created state,
Separation then introduces us to,
The illusion of hell's dark gate.

Part of the Mystery is about remembering,
Part of the Mystery is about balance here,
Part of Ascension is recognition and acknowledgment,
Of our magnificence once illusion clears.

The Trinity is often misunderstood,
To be something it is not,
So much incomplete information,
Because we sleep and we forgot.

The Trinity, the glorious Trinity,
Male, Female and Love,
Love whom men have called the Christ,
As below now so above.

Janine Palmer (Silver Moon)

Mystery's Kiss

The steps up the mountain are challenging and steep,
The treasures of the heart are mysterious and deep,
Tried are we by their misperceptions and lies,
The manifestations of their unknown disguise.

The roads are crooked with twisted beliefs,
And of our happiness they become a thief,
Feeling wounded when maybe we're not,
Things we don't release because our truth we forgot,

Step after step and stone after stone,
After each initiation do we atone,
Higher and higher we climb out of the mists,
Where things are hidden by Mystery's kiss.

The more she detached, the stronger she became,
Strengthening weaknesses so they could not maim.
Healing wounds creates astounding powers,
Nourishing the soil of the collective flower.

Janine Palmer (Silver Moon)

Disclose the Mystery

Bits and pieces of the Mystery,
Flow through you and I,
Each sharing glimpses of memories restored,
As parts of our ego triggers die.

As we awaken to remember,
As we awaken to recognize,
As we begin to see through the illusion,
We begin to shed the disguise.

As we muster our intelligent power,
As we apply our greater strength,
We begin to take our divine power back,
When from our inner truth we drink.

Along this journey we learn things,
And so we must unlearn,
When we are re-directed back to our own divine truth,
For the outer we will no longer yearn.

Each with their own perceptions,
Opinions will always change,
When more and truer knowledge is added,
We are always reading or writing a page.

The Mystery is the quest,
The search for knowledge gained,
The wisdom we seek is within us,
Just waiting there to be claimed.

But first we must now unsubscribe,
To the falsehoods upon which we feast,
To stop trying to gather the temporary illusion,
When within us is the spiritual yeast.

The Mystery contains things unseen,
The Mystery flickers in and out of you and me,
The mystery is why do we accept false fairytales?
Which are shackles when we are free.

The Mystery is the greatest power,
The Mystery is love not described,
The love is where we come from,
And we grow from it when we imbibe.

Janine Palmer (Silver Moon)

haze

Through the haze are treasures hidden,
Through the haze are things which test,
Through the haze you might find peace,
Through the haze is suffering and unrest.

Through the haze by freewill choice,
Our realities here we create,
The consequences of our decisions,
Determine the direction and the gates.

The haze might make us hesitate,
The haze might cause us fear,
But through the haze are treasures,
On the other side of fear our love is clear.

The mysterious cloud of unknowing,
The Mystery of the illusion and the veil,
The Mystery of forgetting our origins,
The Mystery of creation where love shall prevail.

The Mystery of descending to this lower plane,
The Mystery of the magic we contain,
The Mystery of what we forgot,
As we remember, Ascension is gained.

But to rise we must let go of ideologies,
Like the cutting of the puppet's tight strings,
Beliefs are some of the strings to the puppets,
Holding us back from what our inner knowing brings.

The haze is just a temporary fog,
Which we can blow away,
When we rise above egoic group think,
To the truth, the light and the way.

Janine Palmer (Silver Moon)

Mystical & Sacred

A Goddess's Prayer

Upon this earthly journey,
God's grace is never apart,
To guide me through compassion's fire,
Whether heavy or light of heart.

The eternal spring of love is present,
Though sadness often intrudes,
But gratitude and happiness,
Are always frequent interludes.

Help me strengthen areas of weakness,
With all I am to bear,
Through my works thy deep love flows,
I know thee hears my prayers.

Work through me on this wretched plane,
Work through me with thy words,
To assist me in these endeavors,
With the strength of my mighty sword.

Blessed and thankful are they who would listen,
To the whispers of their heart's display,
When anger and wrath will they spurn,
In love's power do they slay.

In gratitude I kneel,
With my sword held fast in my hand,
While all the wounds bleed and heal,
As we unite at thy command.

Sometimes my heart is melting love,
Sometimes it's a bullet so strong,
Sometimes it smiles in happiness,
Sometimes it's sadness's song.

Sometimes I am faced with hatred,
Sometimes it feels like war,
Sometimes I meet the grace in mankind,
Sometimes I find new doors.

The glorious beauty of humanity,
Mixed in with the dregs of hell,
Dark and light and where is the balance?
Within us balance should dwell.

The beasts there and the beauty,
Exulted before thy throne,
Stumbling through a nightmare,
Through awakening they atone.

The washing away of illusion,
Unworthiness flung into the fire,
And the lies religions believed and taught,
Disconnected them from thy spire.

How my love for thee does sing,
Sparks dance forth from thy crown,
Saints long buried now arise,
Like sweet incense from the ground.

The chosen ones to lead them,
Out of the darkness of their plight,
Toward a love so indescribable,
Toward the love which glows as light.

The words of thee through many come,
The flow of grace to earth,
As we rise in our ascension,
Through the process of rebirth.

No more will we suffer ignorance,
No more shall we be slaves,
To religious or political ideologies,
Which line illusion's graves.

In grace and heartfelt gratitude,
The goddess kneels as truest friend,
For the opportunity now to serve,
To teach, to heal, to mend.

To defend the very needed things,
The warrior's path in grace,
Whether received with compassion's brilliant truth,
Or whether faced with hatred's painful face.

Tears which fall like diamonds bright,
From the sadness in my heart,
Cleanse my soul through compassion's spring,
Because from the All we never part.

Gratitude the sweetest elixir,
It heals and fuels my course,
Love for and from my brethren,
The balance of Mystery, a curious force.

The windows of the individual,
In which God can always be seen,
The love which flows, known and unknown,
Through life's mysterious stream.

In gratitude with my broadsword,
I serve thee in compassion's grace,
And the love I share with humanity,
Is the smile upon my face.

The sword represents the power,
The sword represents divine strength,
It is used to cut away what no longer serves,
So healing waters we may drink.

The balance so needed in between,
The Divine Masculine and Divine Feminine here,
Something so far out of balance,
In so many cultures and religions for too many years.

The Divine Feminine is rising to nurture,
For balance to be so restored,
A coming together of hearts and souls,
As we lay down our swords.

Janine Palmer (Spirit Silver Moon)

Of My ~

The dragon of my intention,
Breathes life into wisdom's bright realm,
Into parts of me which exist in slumber,
To the pockets of treasure, where truth still dwells.

The aspects of my Goddess,
Flickering in and out of here and now,
The queen of my transformation here,
And my angel shows me how.

Memories of my golden throne,
Which accompanies me wherever I go,
And the strength I gain when battles are won,
From the illusions I overthrow.

The purity of my horses,
Which carry me hither and yon,
Who guide me through my journey,
No matter what path I am on.

The beauty of my ancient trees,
And the wisdom they provide,
The guidance from them whenever I ask,
And from nothing do they hide.

The water of my spirit,
And the water of the earth,
Flowing ever flowing in movement,
Through the course of my rebirth.

And the sparks of my divinity,
Which light my way now and before,
Are the lamps which light my path back home,
Now and forevermore.

Janine Palmer (Silver Moon)

Mystical Order

Many things are mystical,
Seeds which were planted in us,
To germinate, sprout and blossom,
When we open to love and trust.

To trust the truth we find within,
To step out of dogmatic control,
To our true and pure purpose and power,
As we fan the ember of our soul's deep glow.

To awaken to sacred wisdom,
Ancient and holy and true,
Outside sources might spark awareness of it,
But it exists within me and you.

The order of our higher being,
The order of tranquility and grace,
The pure essence of divine spirit,
You might see flicker across a face.

The vibration of someone familiar,
Part of your soul tribe you know,
Who nurture your soul through dark nights here,
As above now so below.

Janine Palmer (Silver Moon)

Warrior's Door

The bones of the ancestors might be reminders,
Of the paths they walked before,
But the part of them which never dies,
Walks on through the warrior's door.

Mystical and ancient legends of Truth,
Some are understood and some are not,
Some things are known or unknown,
And on this level some we forgot.

The ravens are mystical messengers,
Keepers of wisdom and lore,
The spirits of the animals which guide us,
Now and forevermore.

And the dove reminds us of our spirit,
If we listen to the whispers on high,
As we rise above dogma's illusions,
Back to our power now by and by.

The dragons whom we can no longer see,
But which many of us can still feel,
Compared to the illusions we exist in here,
Are far more compassionate and real.

Though good and bad like everything here,
The light and shadow of all,
And the work we do here in this realm,
To heal the ignorance of the fall.

The warrior men and women,
Who are spoken of in history,
Are here again to carry on their work,
Do you know they are you and me?

And through the ropes and knots,
The cultures and bits of wisdom in between,
Sifting through the wheat and the chaff,
For the enlightenment we must glean.

The stories and lore which remind us,
When they inspire us with memory's spark,
And so we see a glimmer of light,
Which soon guides us out of the dark.

The armor of our ancestors,
Their experiences are part of us,
Part of our indwelling immortal spirit,
Not connected to any bones in the dust.

Janine Palmer (Silver Moon)

Sacred Land

The connection to the mother,
Through beings from elsewhere,
The roots and branches connecting the two,
As we rise up to our castle's lair.

Reconnection with the truth now,
Of who we really are,
And why we ventured to this plane,
Through so many planets and the stars.

But this land is ever sacred,
With our ancestor's blood it's so drenched,
And only when we step out of illusion's realm,
Will our search for truth finally be quenched.

Listening so very intently,
To what mother earth and the creatures say,
And also listening to our heart speak,
As Great Spirit and our ancestor's guide our way.

But don't we all learn by experience?
We love this land where we currently live,
But this land is not where we come from,
And we must give back to her what she gives.

We must endeavor to find balance,
On earth and in our heart and soul,
To juggle the lessons and the rewards,
Which help to strengthen our inner glow.

Sacred for our ancestor's sake,
A great home to the initiates here,
Who love and honor this sacred land,
Through our time travel through the mysteries of fear.

The fear(s) we are meant to conquer,
As warriors we become,
When we face the initiate's challenge(s),
And overcome them with the power of One.

This sacred land is a testing ground,
This sacred land so blessed,
And our bodies here are sacred garments,
Which we wear here to pass the tests.

Janine Palmer (Silver Moon)

Cherished

I cherish the beauty of ancient trees,
Their fragrance, their beauty and shade,
Their wisdom and treasures they share with the world,
Anchoring the heavens and earth, which Creation made.

I cherish the bodies of water,
The life force, the beauty, the sound,
The rivers and streams, veins of lifeblood,
From the rain clouds to pools on the ground.

I cherish the winds of spirit,
The storms and the breezes which blow,
And the whispers of our ancestors as we listen,
While we continue to evolve here and grow.

I cherish the love of this world,
I cherish the love of realms afar,
Closer than we think, connecting all of us,
Whither and wherever they are.

I cherish the love here shown to me,
I cherish the beings who have shared,
Who have shared the love of their hearts and souls,
Who were open and brave, who dared.

I cherish the connections of love I have,
I cherish the gifts of love given to me,
I cherish the reconnections so deeply felt,
Which will always be mine to keep.

I cherish the parents and the children,
Who give while they suffer on their paths,
Who teach of love through tears and pain,
Who find treasures amongst the lack.

I cherish all whom I have been,
I cherish my experiences and knowledge gained,
I cherish the wisdom I hold and the love of God,
I cherish my guides and angels who love me without restraint.

I cherish Gaia the mother,
Mother Nature's bounty gracefully bestowed to us here,
I cherish the whispering guidance of the Holy Spirit,
As She helps those who listen to find their truth more clear.

Janine Palmer (Silver Moon)

Angels

Floating in and out of the clouds,
Twinkling between light and dark,
Glimpses of the moon in and out of the dream,
Are remnants of God's own spark.

Thunder claps in the distance,
Or something rumbling quite near,
Bright flashes of brilliant lightning,
And for a brief moment things are so clear.

Moonlight illuminated so mystically,
Behind the shadow of the clouds,
Winds which blow in softest breeze,
Or in gales strong and loud.

He floated along by force of wings,
On a mission straight from God,
To bring enlightenment and healing,
Through experience, deed and thought.

To help clear away illusion,
To disconnect programs which hinder so much,
To sweep our temples frequently,
Free from any crutch.

To free from us the falsehoods,
Which have so many in their grip,
To come into alignment with our truth,
Along our paths we slip.

To whisper to us gently,
Is what our angels do,
What we gain is wisdom and truth,
When we allow it to come through.

He is a being of brilliant light,
Twinkling on waves of Grace,
And if you could see him with physical eyes,
You would recognize his face.

Janine Palmer (Silver Moon)

Boots and Tunics

Angels with boots and tunics,
Dance in realms around,
Some carry swords or scriptures,
They are treasures to be found.

Some are defenders and protectors,
Some are teachers and guides,
Some are healers from the realm of divine love,
In rays of light do they abide.

Quietly do they whisper,
But not everyone can hear,
Always are they present,
When asked to dry a tear.

Written upon our sacred scrolls,
Agreements forged in light,
Tests for us to remember divinity,
Our truth, our light and our might.

Some people though do not believe,
But that didn't change the fact,
That the angels are guardians with us,
Protectors at our back.

Teachers of sacred knowledge,
Angels in God's service now,
Archers of discovery,
If we let them show us how.

Janine Palmer (Silver Moon)

Divine Wisdom & Energy

Energy Field

Energy is all around us,
Created and then shared,
From thoughts and actions around us,
From the things which our souls bear.

The energy of love from the heart,
The energy of pain experienced from loss,
The energy of ego and judgment,
When we don't rise above the dross.

What energy do you create here?
What energy do you share?
How do you show love for your brethren?
How do you show that you care?

Energy positive or negative,
In what way does it serve?
Does it create good or bad?
Does it help or hinder your verve?

Energy does not go away,
But it can be transmuted and healed,
Love is the most powerful force in creation,
The most powerful energy field.

Janine Palmer (Silver Moon)

Focused Energy

Focused energy is creative,
It is powerful and strong,
Will you create good with it?
Or will you do some wrong?

Whatever you focus your thoughts on,
Is what you will create,
So will you create from a place of love?
Or will create from hate?

Will the remnants of your unhealed wounds,
Come forth with toxic rage?
To harm another along your path,
Or will you rewrite that page?

Always take the wisdom gained,
From any experience, good or bad,
Then peel away the old skins,
To reveal happy as you release the sad.

Transform your energy through healing,
Transform through your own inner grace,
To transform the world around you,
Starting with the smile upon your face.

Janine Palmer (Silver Moon)

The Divinity Field

Call it out by its name,
And whither does it answer?
Does it stand in the light of its own truth?
Or is it darkness's puppet dancer?

Will you challenge a thing,
If it so challenges you?
Will you learn from it or resist it?
Does your divine power blaze new trails through?

Do you clear out denser energies?
Do you create things which resonate so true?
Are your actions an accurate reflection,
Of the essence of the beauty of you?

Your energy is your sacred space,
Stand in your power with divine love all around,
With boundaries for respect and balance,
And peace and power will abound.

The strength which is part of your being,
Resonating all around like a shield,
Where love flows in and out in beauty,
Through the wonder of the divinity field.

Janine Palmer (Silver Moon)

Knights of the Order

Sacred knights of different realms,
Dispatched to assist the cause,
To help man rise out of the quagmire,
Forgetting as they have our spiritual laws.

Not the misinterpreted laws,
Not the creations of so many things by man,
But the spirit waiting on quiet wings,
Inside and unheard because they don't understand.

Too many distractions in their midst,
As illusions dance their destructive dance,
While man creates pain and suffers from it,
Not giving the voice of spirit a truthful chance.

The knights and angels of the order,
Watch man dance in and out of shadows all around,
They can't interfere because of man's free will,
But when man steps out onto the path, new treasures abound.

New doors are waiting to open,
With clues and keys for the game,
And when man begins to open to his inner truth,
The quality of his life won't be the same.

In the naked light how shadows dance,
They show us things in different light,
White light reflects all colors and rays,
Dark absorbs them distorting our plight.

Certain things are captured,
In scriptures, songs and poems,
In stories told or written,
Which connect us back to home.

So many feelings and emotions,
Of history's experience now,
Whether history is repeated or not,
We experience by our agreements and vows.

After initiations things can be revoked,
They can be cut away, removed or burned,
They can be healed, shifted or restored,
As new pages are written or turned.

The Knights and Angels are ever watching,
And the knights are also we,
The knights are the pillars of all the rays,
In us and so always free.

Janine Palmer (Silver Moon)

Chainmail

Links of element's pieces,
Connected one by one,
Through skill and toil for purpose,
The battle had begun.

Accumulated for protection,
Accumulated for power,
To protect divinity's vehicle,
The exterior perimeter of the tower.

He carried the weight of the mail,
To deflect incoming hurtful things,
Protection for his earthly temple,
From the pain of beings whose hearts can't sing.

One day he removed the chainmail he wore,
It fell to a heap on the ground,
And there he dropped his sword as well,
He walked toward other things now waiting to be found.

He never looked back toward the battles,
He walked away from the anger and hate,
He went deep into the wilderness,
Where he entered through divinity's gate.

He entered into another realm,
While still existing on this earth,
He shed all of his fear and worry,
He shed hatred and anger for rebirth.

He cared not for religion,
If it required him to fight his brother, it was not true,
He would serve no one here and nothing,
But his soul where God came through.

He was in peace with nature,
With the animals and plants around,
And if he was very still and quiet,
He could hear the sweetest sounds.

Sometimes he could hear the angels,
He could hear their singing choirs,
He prayed every day at nature's altar,
In gratitude for blessings, continuing to transpire.

The sound of the babbling brooks,
Would speak to him every day,
And in that space of tranquility,
He found the truth the light and the way.

Chainmail while protective,
Would serve him here no more,
For by choice and in his own power,
He walked out of shadow's door.

Janine Palmer (Silver Moon)

Connective

Different tribes connected to the collective,
Different experiences of the same,
Tribes tested to rise above this illusion,
In this challenging earth school game.

Some tribes will work together,
Some tribes will war and fight,
Until they rise above and conquer the ego,
Defending the illusions of wrong and right.

Mankind here stumbles in the shadows,
Until he learns his truth he doesn't need to defend,
That his truth cannot be taken from him,
When he rises above the lies of falsehood and sin.

When the tribes recognize they are worthy,
That they are the blessed innocence of their souls,
Then they kindle the greater collective fire,
And brighter the earth light glows.

Janine Palmer (Silver Moon)

Transformative Fire

Torched

He torched her with the dark fire,
Of his words which formed from thoughts,
He singed the love she carried for him,
Because her honor he apparently forgot.

What possessed him to think the worst of her?
What possessed him to believe such lies?
What possessed him to endeavor to be so unkind?
Why did he remove his disguise?

Which part really was the disguise?
What it the dark or was it the light?
And how was she to determine now,
If how she felt was wrong or right?

What happens when we don't like the shadow side?
Or what appears from behind the mask?
What happens when our illusions are shattered?
After life delivers another bitch slap?

We must be able to forgive,
Or this gauntlet we will not survive,
We rise and soldier on with bandaged wounds,
In order that we might thrive.

We must see past the shadow side,
Past the behaviors of others which main,
But due to the damage we endure,
Some things don't remain the same.

There are types of love so very deep,
And parts of that will always remain,
But it might take a while to pull out the shards of shrapnel,
And to clean up the wounds and the stains.

The pieces which do pierce our hearts,
Sometimes they go very deep,
And memories remain in the scar tissue,
Which cause hesitation as it weeps.

When patterns continue to reappear,
When you can see the monster coming in,
You must slam the door in the bastard's face,
And retreat to your lion's den.

Step away from the foulness,
When you see it coming your way,
Pick up your sword and beat it back,
Stand in your power never to sway.

Stand in your honor alone if you must,
Bar and lock that door,
Because the dark is not welcome in your house,
The love you share should be abused no more.

Janine Palmer (Silver Moon)

Twinkle

There was a twinkle of recognition,
Like the reuniting of two old friends,
But then the ragged things they carried,
Reared their heads to make amends.

There was karma to be balanced,
There were fears and pain to be drawn out,
Things to face and conquer,
And demons to turn out.

There were weaknesses to strengthen,
And so drama did ensue,
The way we react or respond due to patterns,
When we try to block pain from coming through.

When the pain tries to come out,
It's not a pretty sight,
And when faced with yours or another's,
It will test your mettle and your might.

The reuniting of soul connections,
From lifetimes long gone by,
Might only last a very short while,
To help us release the tears we need to cry.

Some will last eternities,
In loving and positive ways,
It all depends on how we nurture them,
Do we give them life or dig their graves?

When we dig another's grave,
We also dig one of our own,
The tedious thing about this challenging life;
Welcome to the free will zone.

Everyone has free agency,
The ability to create by choice,
Cause and effect and consequence,
Words are created by the tone of our voice.

What you create for another,
You will have to taste for yourself,
So will you create heaven, my love?
Or will you create an inferno of hell?

The thing about an inferno,
Is that fire is pure and true,
It will burn away and transmute,
What isn't good for you.

And then what will you plant in the ash?
What wisdom from knowledge, what seeds?
And how will the ash of the sacred fire,
Grow for you what you need?

Janine Palmer (Silver Moon)

Divine Fire

He walked with a blade of honor,
He carried it to cut away things which bind,
He used it on his journey to help enlighten,
Those who were spiritually blind.

He was forged from great fire,
And from fire his weapon was made,
A sword of strength to do his work,
Where sometimes he needed a blade.

When he cut away restricting ties,
From things along the journey which hinder,
Severed to assist in rising above,
Freed from the fire of the blade to tinder.

The fire of the blade so pure,
The fire to burn away the dross,
The fire to burn the ropes away,
Which bind them to their cross.

We are forged in cosmic fire,
Our spirit of love and light,
And now we exist in amnesia,
In the dualistic idea of wrong and right.

Somehow we must cut or peel away,
The masks, illusions and veil,
To disconnect from the falsehoods here,
To break free from the nails.

Somehow to begin to remember,
Our divinity and our worth,
As we walk through hellfire and initiations,
Through the experience of our rebirth.

What part of you is divine fire?
Do you recognize your might?
As well all struggle to maintain balance,
Between the shadow and the light.

He continued to burn through binding ties,
With the light of the sword he saw through,
To the truth within his own soul,
Pointing the way to what he must do.

The fires of creation and manifestation,
The fires of destruction for rebirth,
Our connection to the Divinity of Heaven,
And our connection to Mother Earth.

To be grounded here to the Mother,
To spirit and matter so strange,
To be connected to two realms and integrate,
To ascend from things far deranged.

To recall our infinite connection,
Part of us is eternal and part of it dies,
The physical body is a suit of clothes we wear,
As we cut our way out of the lies.

To discover the truth of our divinity,
To know our spirit ever lives on,
To recognize our own power here,
To no longer be a pawn.

The power of the sword comes from him,
The power of fire is creation,
And when he discovered that God is in him.
He existed in grant elation.

Janine Palmer (Silver Moon)

Coals

The coals catch light with kindling,
They are stoked as they glow through heat,
They glow with warmth into embers,
The process of transformation to repeat.

The orange glow of the fire,
Whether the flame is seen or not,
The beauty of the color there,
Is a thing not soon forgotten.

And as they eventually burn down,
To the finest pile of ash to sit,
The energy expended, witnesses and absorbed,
Is something we will not soon forget.

What do we think as we watch them?
Glowing in the hearth somewhere,
How the mind wanders to mysterious things,
Of secret longing and the love we have shared.

How the coals have warmed men through time,
To carry on with their earthly deeds,
And such a place of transformation,
Man uses for kindling of any unwanted weeds.

And that ash might nurture new growth,
Added to the soil for rebirth to assist,
Amazing the things which rise from the ashes,
Things which flourish from things that are spent.

Janine Palmer (Silver Moon)

Purification by Fire

Through lessons, experiences and fire,
The purification of fire for good,
And the Masters in the background helping her,
When she peeked out from behind her hood.

Sometimes we don't recognize a good thing,
Before we push it away,
Before our old wounds come up to test us,
We lash out and maim and slay.

And the pain we inflict and share,
Has a ripple effect you see,
It branches out to keep delivering pain,
Until by our own power we become free.

The destruction we encounter is necessary,
To break away the old marble and shells,
To free ourselves so we can rebuild,
A new part of ourselves apart from hell.

Some say to subdue your passion,
But that depends on one's perspective,
Passion in the old language is suffering,
Or it can mean a driving force more reflective.

Subduing your passion might be subduing what controls you,
It might be a way of taking your power back,
From thoughts or pain or memories,
To get you back on track.

But the passion that is the driving force,
The passion of your compassionate flame,
That must be fanned with divine love,
To do your work for greater good's gain.

So it depends upon interpretation,
It depends on what is in your heart,
Even if others don't see it and throw stones at you,
Let no one dampen your spark.

If your passion is suffering,
Because you lack important facts,
Look within yourself for the answers,
And fill yourself with what you lack.

If your passion is suffering due to another,
This must be subdued for peace,
For you to gain control over false thought-forms,
To find your truth, your wisdom and strength.

If your passion is your calling,
The work you do here for God,
Then you must don your divine armor,
And allow no one upon it to trod.

Become very aware of perspectives,
Become very aware of mirrors,
Become very aware of what is theirs or yours,
And remember we are cleansed by our tears.

Be in gratitude for painful initiations,
Which force you to rise above,
Be aware of the importance of balance here,
Between the raven and the dove.

One of the most important things,
The initiate here does learn,
Is that our God of love has nothing to do with religion,
He/She is a fire in us which burns.

She peeked out from behind her cloak,
Where she observed the workings of man,
Where she took shelter from their pain the threw at her,
And she drew things in the sand.

She sat with her compassion,
She pondered what she continued to learn,
She knew her connection to Creative Source,
Was nothing she must earn.

Janine Palmer (Silver Moon)

The Smoke

The fragrance of the smoke as it rises,
Connects me to the roots of the earth,
As it makes its way to the heavens,
It connects me there, where I came from first.

Earth is where we come to,
Not where we hail from,
We came here as very brave warriors,
For the gauntlet we need to run.

But so many are far too attached,
To the physical world they see,
Not remembering their origins due to illusion,
And then you see they're not free.

So attached to illusion and falsehood,
So attached to the spaceship Earth,
Where we come to learn and evolve,
Through the ashes of our own rebirth.

The aroma of the transformative smoke,
For burning and purification,
Transmuted to energy unseen,
Things created from thought and manifestation.

The smoke can be used for healing,
For sending messages, goodwill and prayers,
To cleanse, release and purify,
To call in and blessings, ours and theirs.

The fires of transmutation,
On the smoke the stories are told,
Carried on to the ancestors,
Through silver, white and gold.

Janine Palmer (Silver Moon)

Phoenix Tears

The burning fires of transformation,
Contained in the phoenix's tears,
Come from burning away the old,
From rebirthing with wisdom beyond the fears.

We burn through life's experiences,
We rise above our very own ash,
We take the wisdom from the challenges,
Keeping the wheat and burning the chaff.

And the things of lower vibrational energy,
Which keep us stuck in any way,
Like guilt and fear and pain and anger,
Are types of demons we must slay.

Although 'demon' might be a misinterpreted word,
Most don't know what it really means,
A divinity or supernatural being between humans and gods,
That is 'daemon' from ancient Greek belief.

But most understand demons to be something evil,
Something which challenges us we must overcome,
And in that context it's very important,
That for ourselves we are the one.

Carrying any unforgiveness,
Is a ticket to earthly hell,
And when you step out of it,
You ring the angel's bell.

Those tears might burn for a while,
Before they are set to flame,
Until you rise above to take your power back,
From this challenging earthly game.

The flame is the purifying force,
The flame is the transformative fire,
A type of baptism and renewal,
For our souls here to transpire.

Tears are cleansing in many ways,
Tears are a form of blessed relief,
When we release them and let the energy flow,
Those burdens don't become such a thief.

Janine Palmer (Silver Moon)

Forms of Healing & Forgiveness

On this Journey

Healers are sent to this dimension,
To help others here to heal,
But they will not be recognized by everyone,
And their light some might try to steal.

On this particular journey,
Like so many others before,
She walked with grace and compassion,
While projectiles came by the score.

What called to her heart and soul was to help heal,
To comfort those who suffered and to bring a little joy,
To uplift the downtrodden wherever she could,
From feelings of pain and anger which continued to destroy.

The effects of these were sometimes directed at her,
Their tar they threw her way,
Jealousies and stored hatred coming out,
Negative energies which slay.

Misperceptions kindled their pain,
False thoughts and accusations, creating false beliefs,
And so they threw stones at her in anger,
Their hatred became a debilitating thief.

Stones and arrows they threw at her,
Spears and daggers and mud and tar,
Needing what she had to offer them,
They just kept creating more karma and more scars.

The one who wanted to help them,
The one who cared about their plight,
They pushed her down into the mud,
And stabbed her with their knife.

They didn't know how to release their anger,
They didn't know how to release their pain,
They didn't know how their hatred fueled them,
And so they stumbled on in lack instead of gain.

Other healers would help her,
To pull the spears from her heart,
To lift her to her tired feet,
To make another start.

Sometimes we have to allow ourselves to receive,
From a place where there is nothing to compare,
Nothing to try to take from someone,
Leaving them abused and stripped so bare.

What do we gain by harming another?
Creating an imbalance while the Lords of Karma look on,
Hopefully we learn from these experiences,
And from somewhere deep in our being, compassion will respond.

When you see a being who is being abused,
Can you image yourself in their position there?
Would you lift a hand to put a stop to it?
Or stand there in pack mentality, acting as if you don't care?

Do you take any pleasure from causing another to suffer?
Because you better be aware that you will experience what you create,
Do you take any pleasure from the suffering of another?
Do you find in yourself more love or more hate?

Do thoughts and fears continue to plague you?
Do you feel like you stand in your power strong?
Or do you feel like your thoughts control you like demons?
Stealing the breath of love from your heart's song?

Life will cause you to change your perspective,
But not if you continue to sleep,
Not if you hide from your truth,
And continue to cause innocents to weep.

To find any peace within yourself,
You must be able to forgive others and your lower self as well,
That is how you will find the door you need,
To let yourself out of hell.

Janine Palmer (Silver Moon)

Tool

What do we call hatred and anger?
What do we call the unhealed pain?
Does it lean more towards light or dark?
Or does it have a name?

There is darkness which is comforting,
On the other end of light,
And there is darkness which is ignorance,
Like a gaff when it does strike.

How on earth does a being heal?
When it can't let go the pain?
When it can't find itself in forgiveness?
Then balance it cannot gain.

First it must forgive itself,
Before it can forgive another,
And if this cannot be achieved,
There is no honor for thy brother.

No honor for the self,
If forgiveness cannot be achieved,
Because unforgiveness is a prison,
Where the howling of the soul can't be released.

Forgiveness is the most powerful tool,
To take one's power back,
The key to balance and happiness,
Which so many beings now lack.

Janine Palmer (Silver Moon)

Truth and Strength and Might

How many languages are there?
How many languages do you speak?
What energy do you carry?
And how often do you weep?

How do you let your wounds bleed?
Through words or thoughts or deeds?
Do repetitive thoughts create hungry programs?
You must feed which always leak?

Any thoughts you give your power to,
Might become your master in some foul way,
Until you can learn to release the rubbish,
Which you have allowed in your energy to stay.

Invite the old false stories,
The things which you misunderstood,
To leave you once and for all,
To go the light to be changed for the good.

And when you release dark energy,
Remember to replace it with light,
Remember to walk with your warrior,
In your own truth and strength and might.

Janine Palmer (Silver Moon)

Healing Glow

She wrote from the love which flowed through her,
She wrote what came from her heart,
Some people didn't understand it,
To some it was a healing dart.

It spoke to the souls of so many,
But some would choose to take offense,
Some would like to find fault in the attempt,
And to her it would make no sense.

She continued to write through any criticism,
She continued to write through so much positive response,
She did it because she was God's warrior,
Whether they believed it or not.

It was not her business what they believed,
It was her business to write what she felt,
It was an ancient call from her heart and soul,
Divine messages shared for illusions to melt.

Some would feel it so deeply,
Some would protest and resent,
Some would allow in needed healing,
Some would find fault, some would find bliss.

It's up to the individual,
Whether they find a thistle or a rose,
Whether they would remain in a self-made cell,
Or whether their soul would blossom and grow.

Janine Palmer (Silver Moon)

Prescriptions

Prescribed to us by divinity,
Is nature's healing balm,
Such beauty here indescribable,
To produce peace through stillness and calm.

To put your roots down with the trees,
To detox by releasing the old suffering you hold,
To the earth to be purified and returned to its source,
Which is the work of wisdom so bold.

To cleanse in the sparkling pure waters,
To rinse off any energetic debris,
To refresh and renew your beloved spirit,
So your energy can again flow free.

Whisper to the trees then be silent,
And if you listen closely you will hear,
Guidance and songs of the angel's love,
And dark thoughts from your head will then clear.

This would be one of God's prescriptions,
To use the earth's cherished gifts,
To release the old to make room for the new,
Because it's time for old stagnation to shift.

Part of the prescription is being grateful,
To be thankful for blessings galore,
And part of the prescription is forgiveness,
Which always opens so many new doors.

Janine Palmer (Silver Moon)

Stillness

In stillness is rejuvenation,
In stillness do we create,
In stillness do we allow divinity to flow,
In stillness are so many gates.

When we can be still now,
To allow things simply to be,
Without worrying or feeling the need to take action,
New answers will be revealed to thee.

When we know not what to do,
We need not worry, just take time to be still,
And in that peaceful place of surrender,
We will regroup and open to heal.

Sometimes we will be proactive,
We will be fueled to do and achieve,
Other times when we feel helpless,
We need to be still so we may receive.

Sometimes we need to do nothing,
To not worry, just be still in place,
To allow energy and peace to flow through,
From a higher state of grace.

Janine Palmer (Silver Moon)

Guided

She said that she was guided,
But there were those who did not believe,
They were mired in ego's jealousy,
And didn't want her to achieve.

They didn't care if angels guided her,
They didn't care that she had work to do,
They didn't care that she did it for higher purpose,
They tried to stop her doing what she was meant to bring through.

They threw the tar of the ages,
At her directly from their hate,
But the angels used bullet proof glass,
As a protective wall with and invisible gate.

Because the villains who threw the tar,
Were those who needed her help so bad,
They threw their pain and burdens at her,
Which was often very challenging and sad.

The angels told her she had work to do,
And the people came to her in need,
But they were used to creating pain and chaos,
Upon which they would often feed.

Their stifled pain would fester,
And create more of the debilitating same,
And they would project it at those would help them,
Because they were stuck in patterns which maim.

She would do what she could for the people,
Who would ask and invite healing in,
And those were the ones who would take their power back,
From their continued re-creation of sin.

The ones who would continue the cycle,
The vicious cycle of jealousy and hate,
So intent on their merry-go-round of suffering,
They cannot see an exit or a gate.

But some discover forgiveness,
After first forgiving themselves,
And suddenly a door opens,
Which leads them out of hell.

Forgiving others is part of the key,
To be fully released from any hell,
And not to hold anything painful inside,
Because the pain creates the cells.

Janine Palmer (Silver Moon)

Mirror of Forgiveness

In a dream she entered a garden,
To forgive people for their perceived wrongs,
To rise above the hurtful things they did,
To listen to her heart's sacred song.

In this garden sometimes were angels,
In this garden were sometimes guides,
There to help her heal and release,
Blocks stuck which liked to hide.

A guide in the garden greeted her,
And had her stand before a mirror,
To say the name of whomever she was forgiving,
To see if it was clear.

When she spoke the words of forgiveness,
Of the person with their name,
She was to observe whether any image of them lingered there,
It was time to step away from their blame.

If an image of them still lingered there,
There might still be more to forgive,
But if it was only her image staring back,
It was time to move on and live.

Feelings of closeness often change,
Due to so many differing perceptions,
And when old pain comes out to wound,
One might retreat from it and the other might feel rejection.

We don't often realize our treatment of others,
Some won't seem to take responsibility for their actions,
Twisting their issues and firing them like weapons,
Will always cause or create reactions.

If a person has the self-respect,
And if a person has the strength,
They might need to detach and walk away,
From projectiles created by or creating grief.

With the act of true forgiveness from love,
Certain karma is balanced and done,
And from illusions and merry-go-rounds,
We are no longer drawn to nor do we run.

To stand in our truth and acceptance,
Of who we know we really are,
To have the courage to walk away from what we know is untrue,
Is to avoid the inflicting of many new scars.

The mirror in the garden,
The mirror of the dream,
Will show us the truth when we are ready,
When in acceptance and love we glean.

Janine Palmer (Silver Moon)

Their Return

They return again and again as healers,
From spirit for the spirit, for the ancestors and the land,
Breathing new life into the healing wounds,
Because of the karmic plight of man.

For the healing of the spirit,
For healing of the heart and soul,
For releasing unneeded burdens,
To restore a healthy glow.

To delve into the depths of forgiveness,
For ourselves and also for others,
For healing for the collective,
For our ancestors our sisters and brothers.

For healing for the planet,
Mother earth our temporary home,
To heal those lost in spirit,
From the confusion and sadness where they roam.

To heal the illusion of fear,
To conquer it and burn it in the fire,
To transform so many things for the greater good,
And as we evolve so beauty transpires.

Janine Palmer (Silver Moon)

Fountain of Forgiveness

There is a fountain of forgiveness,
In every man and woman on earth,
It is only found in one place,
Inside each person for rebirth.

The fountain of forgiveness,
Is a magical elixir which so heals,
It heals the wounds and the pain,
And restores the happiness misperception steals.

We can easily access it,
When our heart is stronger than our mind,
When we rise above our ego's offence,
To the peace there we will find.

When we take a step back from our limited perception,
When we let go of the need to be right,
When we stop thinking it's all about us,
When we detach from the need to fight.

When we realize there are things we don't know,
About a person, a place or a thing,
When we learn to take a step back and detach,
It will be more clear and less of a sting.

When we recognize that things happen,
For reasons we don't understand,
Then we free ourselves from a prison,
When in our own power we stand.

When we cease to hold anything against another,
When we cease to hold anything against our self,
That is when the door unlocks and flies open,
That trap door of our cell.

When we drink from the fountain of forgiveness,
It's an elixir of beauty and light,
Which frees us and empowers us,
From the truth or illusion of the soul's dark night.

Janine Palmer (Silver Moon)

The Emotion

Thoughts and sensations ever swirling,
Good or bad, they help us to feel,
Emotions are temporary messages,
But do not store them, lest they steal.

They sweep through us as messengers,
Like winds blow through the trees,
We might learn as they direct us,
But let them go to keep you free.

When they are held onto or buried,
Part of us can become a tomb,
Where pain can create poison which lingers,
Brewing a noxious, toxic stew.

Eventually it will work its way out,
Like a volcano which will erupt,
Burning anything in its way,
Consequences so abrupt.

To learn to release the emotion,
Which might create illusion in you and me,
Is to find the path to freedom,
Rise above the traps now to be free.

Janine Palmer (Silver Moon)

Seemingly Unforgiveable

Things which seem unforgiveable,
Often times are not,
We just don't know all the reasons some things happen,
Because we exist in a realm where we forgot.

We don't see the reasons things happen,
We do not have all the facts,
We don't understand why things happen to test us,
Or how we grow by what we think we lack.

When we hold onto any unforgiveness,
We lock part of our self in a cell,
Where we begin to take up residence,
In a particular type of hell.

In forgiveness there is great freedom,
But first ourselves we must forgive,
Before we can begin to forgive others,
So this sacred life we can live.

Most often here we do not see,
The unhealed wounds festering there beneath,
But we see the ugly effects of them,
As they flow out causing strife and grief.

Experiences in this life will test us,
As we face each initiation's gate,
To rise above resentment and anger,
So we don't fall prey to the energy of hate.

To find the beautiful pieces of love,
Woven in between the suffering and pain,
Is to reconnect with our divinity,
As our sacred strength we gain.

Sacred Shamanic Whispers

Things that seem unforgiveable,
Only appear so due to limited perspective,
If you could see it from higher realms,
You would learn to be more reflective.

The information we lack,
Makes our perspective often confused,
Then we react to misinformation,
Due to illusions so misconstrued.

Of course there are things so painful,
Which are not okay to do,
But when we hold it against another,
It's our own suffering we create anew.

The spiritual law of karma,
Is for balance of any thing,
Where we must experience what we cause or create,
For the wisdom it will bring.

To forgive ourselves through the power of love,
For things we hold against any other,
Is the first step on the path to healing and peace,
As we stand in our power to recover.

In love and scared gratitude,
In light and grace I stand,
I serve through my own divine power,
For the highest Source to assist my clan.

Janine Palmer (Silver Moon)

Meditation

Sometimes we reflect on things very deep,
And sometimes we are distracted,
Sometimes we accept, sometimes we reject,
And we must make room for laughter

Life is a type of meditation,
Designed to make us think,
But we cannot only use the mind,
Through the heart's stream we must drink.

So many have closed their hearts off
Due to experiencing unspeakable pain,
Pain they know not how to process,
So a blockage it remains.

Part of the meditation process,
Is to process and release,
Dark and heavy energy should not stay stuck,
Or else it will become a thief.

Life is a type of prayer,
What type of energy do you bring?
Does it lift and nurture?
Or does it bite and sting?

You may not know how your energy affects others,
Until they reflect it back,
Does it create happiness and joy?
Or does it create suffering and lack?

Joy or strife is determined,
By what we will accept,
And sometimes it is determined,
By what we must reject.

Some people must feel like they deserve,
To be treated like punching bag somehow,
They must know or accept their own worthiness,
By the poor treatment they continue to accept and allow.

Perceptions direct our experiences,
They shape and shift how we feel,
How we respond or react,
Too what is and isn't real.

With the information we gather,
New realities we create,
Is it bathed in light or gloom?
The entrance to your gate?

When we reflect on our feelings,
Our emotions which come and go,
We come away with many tools,
For illusion to overthrow.

Sometimes the behavior of others,
May feel hurtful and boggle the mind,
How much of their behavior is affected by wounds,
Which keep them spiritually blind?

Sometimes people mirror something about us,
Sometimes we don't like,
So we might take it out on that person,
Wielding a protective knife.

Sometimes people project their issues,
They twist things around to pin them on us,
It is very destructive behavior,
Coating our shackles with layers of rust.

Part of us is a sacred wolf,
Liston when to the moon it howls,
There are things in need of acknowledgement,
We are the masters of our trowels.

What do we do with this life?
Is it about material things?
Is it about our part in the Mystery?
How we listen to our soul when it sings?

The parts of us angelic,
The vibrations of light and sound,
But also very important,
To be rooted to the ground.

Life is a type of meditation,
You get out of it what you put in,
Are you adding salt or sugar?
By what you defend or offend?

Have you found some neutral ground?
Beyond the realm of taking sides?
Can you allow your brother to be who he is?
Without opinions and perceptions which chide?

The energy of God experiences itself,
Through us on Earth's space ship,
What energy comes out of our mouths from our minds?
Is it honey or venom that drips?

Janine Palmer (Silver Moon)

Ascension & Spiritual Alchemy

Thistle and Weeds

He discovered her one day while out walking,
There in the midst of the thaw,
Covered in roses amongst the thistle and weeds,
And there he stood in awe.

He knelt to place a hand upon her,
As she began to stir,
And the most amazing thing he witnessed,
Was an ethereal light there glowing from her.

He had always been a seer,
And suddenly he was shown,
Her plight was the plight of the world,
To be healed now as it became known.

Acknowledgment of the Divine Feminine,
Because here and now she was coming back,
Because the time had come from Divinity,
To bring in the balance we have so lacked.

He was shown how through ignorance and cruelty,
Due to fear and thirst for control and power,
How mankind had squashed the Divine Feminine,
Disrespecting the womb and the flower.

He was shown a horrible imbalance,
Like a scourge upon the earth,
How mankind has stumbled in suffering and darkness,
Until they experience rebirth.

People can learn from time in the dark,
Where they learn to call in the light,
They learn to re-establish balance,
To take back their power and stand in their might.

Sacred Shamanic Whispers

No one is going to offer it to you,
It is something you must claim,
But a being can't focus on their own needed healing,
While their brethren they continue to maim.

He was shown how some people clinging to religions,
Were and are misled by illusion's clever snare,
Where they believe(d) incomplete and misunderstood truths,
Judging their brethren in ways so unfair.

He was shown the healing and nurturing creation,
Which from the Divine Feminine comes,
But it was so hard for them to receive it from her,
When it was her they continued to shun.

He saw her rising greatly,
Again from the womb of Creation,
Because the time had come again now,
For God's children to know elation.

He was shown how we each have work to do,
To discover our divine truth within,
When we do is when the path opens,
For our Ascension to begin.

He was prompted to lend a hand to her,
To assist her along her path,
Because now he knew it was part of his calling,
To help bring the Divine Feminine back.

Blessings for the balance of the Divine Masculine and Divine Feminine

Janine Palmer (Silver Moon)

her Queen's Speech

Her queen's speech was for awareness,
Awareness of others here,
To do our best not to harm,
Create not in another any harmful tears.

Her queen spoke about compassion,
Her queen spoke of the spirit of grace,
Her queen spoke of people's unhealed wounds,
For which we must hold space.

Her queen spoke to her of tolerance,
Her queen said we must judge not,
Her queen said in the process of finding balance,
Sometimes we're cold and sometimes we're hot.

She said illusions will often fool us,
That things are not usually what they seem,
And when we react to falsehoods,
We miss so many hidden things.

Her queen spoke of needing to find balance,
Her queen spoke of honesty and truth,
She spoke of the truth in each individual,
And the wise man and the fool.

Her queen said to be forgiving,
Her queen said to put all burdens down,
Because when you release what you shouldn't carry,
Is when you gain your crown.

Janine Palmer (Silver Moon)

Tribes

And so the tribes are uniting,
Who once used to war and fight,
Because there is a bigger threat and enemy,
And our Natives are known for standing for what is right.

The battle to sustain earthly grace,
From those controlled by so much greed,
Those who rape the land and the people,
Creating gaping wounds which bleed.

Passed down through the ancestors,
Are things which need to be healed,
But so many hold onto the hate which feeds it,
And their own happiness they then steal.

Stand for what is right,
Stand in strength and truth,
Allow the wisdom of the ancients,
To filter now through you.

Certain agreements have been made,
Which need to be acknowledged and honored,
In their quest for wealth and power,
The ignorant murder their mothers and fathers.

A disgusting display of the lower,
Of lower vibrational hell,
Upon this earth our Mother,
It's time to break the spell.

And we also made sacred agreements,
In spirit before we came here,
To do work through pain for the collective,
To rise above our fears.

Send the light of divine healing,
To the land and the people through power,
To the animals, the guides and the ancestors,
As a new earth begins to flower.

Stand in your divine strength all you warriors,
And do it from a place of calm,
Yes there are things which fuel us,
But hatred is not a healing balm.

Anger can fuel our actions,
But it shouldn't be where we live,
When we identify too much with hatred,
To the opposition our power we give.

Call in the wisdom and the energy,
From the ancestors, spirits and guides,
Send your light to the earth and humanity,
It's in the strength of love where miracles abide.

Share your energy with the earth and draw from her,
And draw from the Creator on high,
For the combination of truth and strength,
Where new blessings come alive.

Many true warriors rise above,
Ideas of hatred and revenge,
By detaching from ideologies,
This is when spirit mends.

The tribes are reuniting,
From the dark all around comes the light,
The tribes are seeking fair balance,
Beyond ideologies of wrong and right.

Peace, blessings, love and light to all warriors

Janine Palmer (Spirit Silver Moon)

Aspects

What is woven into creation?
Things we know and things we don't,
Things unfold and we discover them,
Unless we are closed and then we won't.

To discover the different aspects,
Of ourselves and who we are,
Remnants of who we've been before,
Accumulated wisdom blended with scars.

The parts of us who dance,
The parts of us who weep,
The intricate little nuances,
Things shallow and things deep.

What we brought in with us,
And what we learn here in this time,
The mountains and the valleys,
The things we swim and the things we climb.

Our vibrant gifts we shine here,
And the fears which test our mettle,
The fires which ever transform us,
Through the steam of life's great kettle.

The things upon this curious plane,
Which sometimes burn us to ash,
And the strength we find within to rise above,
And into the fire we throw their lash.

What makes us who we are?
The stones which sharpen the blade,
And the brilliant light of the diamond,
Which the greatest pressure made.

Janine Palmer (Silver Moon)

Sovereign

The sovereign power in any man's reality,
The sovereign power in any man's life,
Is the power of the man himself,
When he removes the illusion of society's knife.

Societies which threaten and bully,
Societies whose egos rage like a bull,
Societies whose ignorance overflows to its people,
Victims of location and circumstance where the shite house is full.

But are they really victims?
Or did they on some other level agree,
To come into a lower vibrational situation,
To learn how to rise above and be free?

Did they descend to learn and remember?
Did they come to learn to remember their power?
Were they planted here like seeds in the shite?
To persevere and to blossom and flower?

To rise above adversity,
To grow through cracks in hard soil,
To find glimpses of happiness and joy here,
Through their hard work, suffering and toil.

And were they to find wisdom here?
And treasures along the way?
Were they to recognize and claim their own worthiness?
And their power again here today?

Janine Palmer (Silver Moon)

Emotions as Teachers

Emotions tell us how we feel,
But actions from them open gates,
We must regain control over reactions,
So we don't get caught up in hate.

Control is mostly illusion,
But we are in charge of our choices and actions,
Unless we give our power away,
By our ego triggered reactions.

To learn not to be offended,
Is ascension on the warrior's path,
To deflect the knives they throw at us,
And to lay down our own gaff.

Emotions can be teachers,
When we feel them and let them flow,
As long as they don't get stuck in us,
Where they can dampen or dim our glow.

Janine Palmer (Silver Moon)

Waves of Love

Feelings of certain kinds of power,
Wash over us flowing out and in,
Sneaking up when least expected,
Directing experiences as they begin and end.

And when vibrations match,
And when those vibrations call,
And the most powerful feelings of love emerge,
Do we rise or do we fall?

Submitting to the greatest feeling,
Of love here on this earth,
Might nurture us in divinity,
Or destroy us for rebirth.

Learning from our experiences,
Not allowing old pain to get caught,
Not allowing wounds to be buried,
Due to perceptions we might have bought.

The love must always flow through,
And part of it will always remain,
It is simply a reminder to us,
Where we came from and by experience we gain.

Janine Palmer (Silver Moon)

Rebirth

While she slept one evening,
He swept in on golden wings,
And in the realm where souls traveled,
He visited her in her dreams.

He came to remind her of his love for her,
He came to support her on her earthly walk,
He came to tell her he was proud of her,
For having the courage to walk her talk.

He came to whisper encouragement,
To keep sharing her compassion as she felt called,
That not everyone would understand the depth of her soul,
And sometimes she would feel abused or mauled.

He said to draw strength from the beauty,
She had begun to notice all around,
He said treasures would continue to present themselves,
Waiting for her discovery to be found.

New light would ever be shining,
On new windows and new doors,
That the time had come since she had separated,
The wheat from the chaff upon the threshing floors.

She had become the glorious phoenix,
She had risen from her own ash,
She was the magnificent product of necessary rebirth,
And she had washed the blood from her sash.

Her sacred heart held all the love,
She needed from and for herself,
For alas she had found the key,
To the gate at the illusion of hell.

She had faced her shadow side,
And come away with balanced light,
She had the strength of the mightiest warrior,
Without the urge to fight.

She would not be toppled,
She was a lantern of great light,
She was part of the divine collective,
She was a reflection of God's love and might.

She came from gentle beauty,
She was a goddess returned to earth,
And the moment that she found her truth,
Was the moment of her own rebirth.

He left her with a kiss of promise,
That they would reunite again very soon,
After she did her work for the greater good,
With the power and light of the moon.

Janine Palmer (Silver Moon)

Your Magnificence & Worthiness

Sweet Soul

Are you ready sweet soul to descend now?
To the lower vibrational realm on earth?
For your soul to unfold and evolve there,
To transform through free agency's fire for rebirth?

This is just a reminder,
That you will remember almost nothing of who you are,
When you pass through the veil into that realm,
From the place of love of the stars.

And you must take with you your ego,
You must take your shadow side,
To test you to find your balance,
To rise above illusions and pride.

Pride meaning the illusion of separation,
Self-righteous traps of the ego's snare,
Anyone who thinks they are superior in any way,
Dances in darkness's lair.

You will forget that you are connected,
To a brilliant collective vine,
Which is evidenced by the false defensiveness,
Of the illusion of yours and mine.

Your journey will not seem easy,
Through many initiations and many tests,
Find the truth within yourself,
And you will always do your best.

Duality is testing ground,
The illusion of wrong and right,
What you learn from choices and decisions,
As you walk though shadow and light.

Sacred Shamanic Whispers

The strength of your spirit when tapped into,
Is a force of amazing power,
And the love from your Sacred Heart,
As it begins to blossom and flower.

Many things are learned from painful situations,
Or by how we perceive them as such,
And don't forget you will need to learn to detach,
From falsehoods others use as a crutch.

That last thing I will leave you with,
Is to remember on some level how much you are loved,
You are a brave warrior to enter into matter,
But with you always are the raven and the dove.

The wisdom of the ancients,
Is stored in your DNA,
Your very own personal library,
And love will guide your way.

Janine Palmer (Silver Moon)

Vicinity

Somewhere in the vicinity of assumed truth,
There are falsehoods woven in,
Whenever we begin to believe,
We are unworthy due to sin.

To learn by experience is the journey,
Making a mistake doesn't necessarily make you wrong,
It does not throw you into a category of unworthiness,
Don't be quick to believe, in falsehood's misleading song.

On higher levels so many things are considered,
Which apply to why people do what they do,
The knowledge of why things happen,
Is not something possessed by me or you.

We make snap judgments erroneously,
We jump to conclusions far too soon,
Too busy worrying about other's mistakes,
To take notice of our own between the sun and the moon.

When we step out of a place of judgment,
And hold nothing against anyone else,
Is when we begin to connect to our wisdom,
And step out of our very own cells.

And similarly we should be aware,
Not to hold anything against ourselves,
At some point along our journeys,
It becomes time to break out of our shells.

Janine Palmer (Silver Moon)

Separation Snare

Forces beyond our comprehension,
How our limited conscious mind works,
So many things we don't understand,
From the viper's pit where fears and insecurities lurk.

Forgetting our Oneness upon our descent here,
The veil of forgetting into duality's state,
Where we begin to believe the illusion we are separate,
And we begin to adopt or get drawn into hate.

How can hate ever be stronger than love?
When our amnesia has become too strong,
And when we begin to judge our brothers,
We've entered a place where we don't belong.

Forgetting our divine origins when we come here,
Forgetting that our magnificence is great,
Instead we get wrapped up in the material world,
And fall through the traps of illusion's gates.

And so it is part of the journey,
Part of such a clever little test,
And how strong then is each warrior?
Who in strength will do their best.

He or she who maintains compassion,
And whoever uses it cannot fail at all,
Compassion creates the divine ladder,
Which helps us reverse the effects of the fall.

Janine Palmer (Silver Moon)

Reverent

The reverent way he looked at her,
Was due to the reverence in her he could see,
He recognized a part of God in her,
A balance we need to be free.

Reverence is a sign to us,
That many people aren't awake enough to see,
Reverence is an aspect of God's children,
Much of humanity will not allow themselves to be.

Too identified with ideologies,
Too identified with the mind,
Not disengaged enough from ego,
To allow ourselves to be kind.

The pyramid of our existence,
And the square which forms our earthly base,
But so many are too busy climbing over their brethren,
In their quest for self, they create error in haste.

Because self is really not separate,
That is the illusion we see,
That is the clever snare here,
Which prevents us from being free.

And then the reverence he saw in her,
He began to see in himself as well,
The more he honored himself and his brethren,
So much more in divine balance did he dwell.

Janine Palmer (Silver Moon)

Sins Against Self

What is the direct translation,
Of the misused words 'to sin'?
It means to miss the mark or miss the point,
Reminding you to try to change your perception again.

Here is a curious question,
How do you sin against yourself?
Believing that you are unworthy,
Is a ticket to self-made hell.

To endeavor to judge anyone on this plane,
Where pure knowledge you do not possess,
Is to keep yourself in stagnation and ego,
And upon your path you will regress.

When you try to numb your buried pain,
With alcohol, drugs or things,
What you bury will fester and choke you,
Until your heart can no longer sing.

When you do not forgive,
Yourself or anyone else,
You sin against your higher self,
Due to the hell where your lower-self dwells.

When you hold onto resentment,
When you hold onto any grief,
It is a terrible sin against yourself,
And of your own happiness you are a thief.

When honesty does not flow from you,
Through the masks you often wear,
When you can't look in the mirror and like what you see,
Therein lie the challenges and the dare.

The challenge is to overcome it,
The challenge is to rise far above,
The secret is to learn balance,
Though the whispers of the raven and the dove.

To love yourself is a golden key,
To love others as yourself as well,
Is a secret key to unlock the door,
To an annoying illusion of hell.

And when you have done this sacred work,
This work for your soul to evolve,
You might find it comes through the love of the Christ within you,
And with deeper understanding you see how it revolves.

And your laughter when you have freed yourself,
Like the tinkling of so many bells,
Is heard in heaven with great rejoice,
When happiness in your heart now dwells.

Janine Palmer (Silver Moon)

Broken Angel

Descending here from a place of love,
Unlike anything on this is earth,
Coming here to help humanity,
With the journey of its rebirth.

But some weren't ready to listen,
Too embroiled in earthly woes,
Too attached to material things,
Stepping on everyone's toes.

Some recognized her compassion,
Some saw things in her she did not,
Some of them held up a mirror to help her remember,
So many things which she forgot.

She was awakening here as well,
From the forgetful sleep of the veil,
She came to remove things which kept them stuck,
Like spiritual coffin nails.

She was guided by higher source,
Her heart and her soul did she heed,
Some of them knocked her to the ground,
And left her heart to bleed.

They threw their filth and tar at her,
They threw their sticks and stones,
Their blood was mixed with her blood,
But she was just a hollow bone.

She was an instrument of the High God,
She was an angel so fair,
She had descended into a type of hell,
Which had now become her lair.

She had to learn to navigate the darkness,
To find the treasures the shadows hide,
She had to speak softly to the awakening ones,
About the others who had lied.

Whether they know it or not,
Falsehoods have been shared,
Keeping man stuck in guilt and shame,
Like fear is now their Laird.

She's there to remind them of their truth,
Which resides in their kingdom within,
She is there to remind them of the true meaning,
Of the translated words 'to sin'.

To sin means to miss the mark,
But so many don't understand,
So many have been programmed to feel unworthy,
Due to the ignorance of man.

Some of them love her deeply,
Some of them are jealous and unkind,
She had to learn to hold her head high,
While she cuts the ties which bind.

Some of them did break her,
But in the dark she found the strength of her wings,
And now she laughs at the folly,
While her sacred heart just sings.

She found her treasure in the shadows,
When she was in the dirt there on her knees,
So many beings were there to help her,
Whom in this realm she couldn't see.

She learned to hear them softly speak,
They spoke directly to her heart and soul,
They helped to mend and heal her,
To kindle her soul's divine glow.

No longer is she broken,
A great love emanates from her heart,
And the origin of the sacred there,
Came directly from God's spark.

Janine Palmer (Silver Moon)

The Compliment of Truth

The dancing vibration of our essence,
At certain points and times we don't see,
The compliment of our divine truth,
Which exists above notions of you and me.

The truth that we are connected,
All created by love so divine,
But we forgot our origins when we descended to earth,
Hidden behind a veil so fine.

The truth within our being,
Is so much more powerful than anything taught in church,
Any perspectives or misperceptions sold,
Which might hinder our divine rebirth.

In the absence of fear if one listens,
They can hear God's voice within,
They can feel the love of who they are,
Above the erroneous notion of sin.

Because the definition or translation of 'sin',
Means simply to miss the mark,
It does not mean that we are unworthy,
Because we are created by God's own spark.

The compliment of the truth of God,
Which exists in every man,
Is the tie which binds all the vines,
Of the beloved soul light clans.

Janine Palmer (Silver Moon)

Holy Fire

Holy fire burns in humanity,
Some see it and some do not,
Some are too busy defending falsehoods,
To realize the lies they have bought.

Holy fire is the pureness,
The innocence of our sacred hearts,
The purity of the depths of our souls,
Where from God we are never apart.

Some are too distracted by the material world,
The lower vibrational circus all around,
Some haven't set foot on their spiritual journeys,
Toward the blessings which abound.

Life will usually toss us around,
For the purpose that we will learn,
To discover the love we need resides in us,
And when we do we will no longer yearn.

Holy fire is God's breath,
Breathed into our souls at creation,
And from that fire we may create,
From our compassion, divine manifestation.

Janine Palmer (Silver Moon)

Forgetful

Oh student of the physical realm,
How do you evolve and grow?
Especially as you have forgotten,
Your magnificence and truth far below.

To forget your place of origin,
To forget other experiences before,
To forget you are an ambassador for God,
Until you rekindle the glow of your soul.

You have forgotten you are divine love,
You have forgotten His love for you,
But by degrees through certain experiences,
You are allowing it to come back through.

But you have not forgotten how to love,
It presents in your gestures and thoughts,
It comes through you in seen and unseen ways,
As above, so below, as sought.

Janine Palmer (Silver Moon)

Come Closer

Come closer to the breath of creation,
Come closer dear to your light,
Lift yourself with gentle loving care,
Step out of your soul's dark night.

Remember these are initiations,
Remember these trails don't last,
Remember you are loved beyond measure,
To heal yourself is the task.

The meek and mild mixed with the warrior,
The warrior so brave and bold,
The knight come here to raise himself,
From battles bought and sold.

To rise above the experience of programming,
To meet God directly in your heart,
Exiting the matrix,
Is it written in your chart?

When your divine spark becomes kindled,
By the hard knocks of this life,
When you're ready to move beyond,
The experiences you create by strife.

Come closer to the love in you,
Come closer for the love in me,
Come closer to unite our flames,
Together we are free.

Janine Palmer (Silver Moon)

Your Beauty

There are many aspects of you,
Some are hidden and some are seen,
Your beauty is your truth and love,
The wisdom gained from who you've been.

Your beauty is an elixir,
A sacred healing balm,
Your beauty in its truest sense,
Is joy and peace and calm.

Your beauty is a healing force,
It is the compassion there from grace,
Many will see it within you,
Or in the familiarity of your face.

Your beauty is the love within,
What fuels the light of your heart,
Your beauty is the love of the All,
From which you never really part.

Your beauty is the love you share,
In kindness and acceptance in flow,
Your beauty comes from being a teacher,
And sharing what you know.

Your beauty comes from experience,
It comes from God in you,
It shines like a sacred beacon,
When you allow it to come through.

Janine Palmer (Silver Moon)

Blessed Be Our Magic

Magical Branches and Roots

Through the trees she walked in solitude,
Acorns scattered upon the forest floor,
But there were so many things unseen there,
So many treasures through so many doors.

There are doors of communication there,
To and from the trees,
Interconnected, anchoring heaven and earth,
And the wisdom which comes from these.

In stillness we might tune in,
To the beauty and healing of these beings,
And if we are open and ask in gratitude,
Guidance will come through for our healing.

To ground ourselves in nature,
A magnificent, nurturing force,
While our spirit connects with divinity,
Combining wisdom and healing of course.

So many birds singing in the trees,
Telling stories we don't comprehend,
Their feathers left as treasures we find,
Once upon a time our ancestors listened to the wind.

Things we have lost through the centuries,
And the things we do now regain,
Our connection with nature, the animals and each other,
Is more of a flow and less of a game.

Here and there are little nests,
Mostly hidden away from our view,
Hidden away for safety,
Blended with the colors of nature's hue.

How the woods replenish the soul,
How nurturing to the spirit it is,
And gratitude flows freely there,
At the wonder of nature's kiss.

Janine Palmer (Silver Moon)

her Magic

He said he could sense the magic in her,
But how could he see things about her which she could not?
There are so many things about ourselves we don't see,
Entering this dimension there is much we forgot.

Intuitive ones would get glimpses,
Of who she was before,
And they are reminders on her journey,
Opening memory's door.

So many friends remind us,
In ways which seem good or bad,
Things we need to know and remember,
About ourselves happy or sad.

The magic is the love,
The magic is the pureness of soul,
The magic is what we hold in our hearts,
And how we use it to fuel our glow.

We might not see our own magic,
Because of how life is designed to drag us down,
So we can find treasure on our knees in surrender,
Buried there in the ground.

The magic which he could see in her,
He began to share with her here,
So she could see another aspect of herself,
In the reflection of him as a mirror.

And she reflected it back to others,
By her thoughts and words and deeds,
Reflecting their worthiness and divine love,
To those whose hearts did bleed.

Sometimes we minister to others,
Sometimes we need to be ministered to,
We must remember to love and trust ourselves,
For our true light to shine through.

Janine Palmer (Silver Moon)

Cauldron Brew

The things of this earth which fill us,
The things we allow into ourselves,
Can create for us a heaven,
Or they can create for us a hell.

What we carry has certain effects,
The things we allow to brew,
The burdens we carry for far too long,
Block new blessings from coming through.

We are a cauldron of our own creation,
What do we carry and what do we release?
Do we let things like anger and pain linger in us?
Do we suffer from distorted dogmatic beliefs?

What nasty things do we toss in,
To the cauldron we carry around?
And what potion does it create until we clean it out,
Does it help us rise above or stay chained here to the ground?

Do you add enough love to your stew?
Do you drain off the parts you don't need?
Are there still remnants from your bleeding heart?
And do you allow it to breathe?

Be aware of what you put in your stew,
Pull out things which don't taste quite right,
Stir it with love and attention,
Until you get the mixture just right.

Janine Palmer (Silver Moon)

Mistress of Magic

She is an enigma to many,
Her spirit so many recognize,
Something familiar about her energy,
Or is it something there in her eyes?

Many aspects woven into her matrix,
Flicking in and out of perception,
Bit and pieces of mystery swirling around,
A flash of memory or some recognition.

Someone they knew so long ago,
Once upon a sacred time,
As we all flow in and out of different realities,
And the magic comes from the vine.

An antediluvian essence so ancient,
Protected by words of the Ancient of Days,
Symbols of ancient wisdom engraved in her aura,
Angels and Masters guide her way.

Once called her the Mistress of Grace,
Her magic of old does she share,
She shares what she knows about healing,
From the ones who laid her bare.

There were those who did not understand,
There were those whom jealousy ruled,
They lashed out in their pain and their anger,
By illusion they seemed to be fooled.

Misperceptions are a cruel master,
Some people just want to be heard,
And when their pain comes bubbling out,
Their vision becomes a bit blurred.

She would hold space for those people,
As best as she could most times,
But sometimes she would have to detach,
And walk away from their crimes,

Sometimes we have to take care of ourselves,
By setting boundaries from and for our power,
So those way-wards don't encroach on our space,
While we nurture and grow and flower.

Her magic was the essence of love,
It was wisdom forgotten to date,
It was God's love flowing through her,
While she navigated their pain and hate.

Divine love is the essence which guides her,
It is the magic which flows from her being,
It's the reason they love her or shun her,
Because of what they are or are not seeing.

The Mistress of Magic and her compassionate flame,
And the mystical fire of her being,
A messenger and scribe for the High God,
Sharing with them tools for their healing.

With gratitude and unconditional love,
With humor and sacred grace,
Sometimes serious, sometimes a warrior,
All etched but sometimes invisible, there upon her face.

A knowing look in her piercing eyes,
A twinkle of love's desire and the Mystery,
They knew they'd known her once upon a time,
Whether the world was enslaved or free.

Janine Palmer (Silver Moon)

The Priestess

The making of a priest or priestess,
No matter how many times again,
Requires periods of great loneliness,
While the spirit expands and bends.

Opening to the wisdom of the Mysteries,
Learning to reconnect with one's soul,
To re-unite with tribes of light,
Ever the widening goal.

To remember the wisdom of the Druids,
Of the tribes people of days of old,
To peel away the layers of modern programming,
To uncover our truth so bold.

To find the Christ within us,
As Christ is not for sale,
And when we answer to the whispers of His love,
The weak breeze becomes a gale.

An energy of love surrounds us,
As we learn and grow and evolve,
And as she reintegrates to her priestess lineage,
Part of the mystery has been solved.

Remembering her magical aspects,
And honoring them on her path,
And by degrees of divine initiations,
Does she take her priestess power back.

Janine Palmer (Silver Moon)

Cathedral of the Forest

She walked with gracious awareness,
Along the trails the animals made,
To a very sacred gathering place,
In a secret, hidden glade.

The trees around this ancient place,
Were of a majesty without any words,
It was like being embraced by nature's arms,
With the love of heaven and earth.

To gaze upon it in wonder,
Takes the mind to many places,
Nature's cathedral has nurtured many souls,
And brought happiness to many faces.

The Cathedral is a place to anchor them,
To heaven and to earth here now,
To come back into right alignment,
Where their hearts will show them how.

The presence of the almighty,
Is always there and also within,
To reconnect to primal truth,
To connect us to home again.

The energy of the magical trees,
And the music through their leaves,
The spirit of the whispering wind,
As sacred as you please.

She gathered berries and twigs,
She gathered leaves and flowers there,
She created things of grace and beauty,
And she wore them in her hair.

A little fox did follow her,
Wherever she would go,
The truest most trustworthy companion.
She had ever known.

Janine Palmer (Silver Moon)

Your Own Honor

her Armor

The armor around her is very strong,
She brought it in with her but strengthened it here,
By experiences in and out of illusion,
By the sheer power of love we find dear.

The armor like boundaries to do her work,
A field of light to heal or deflect,
To share divine energy here through love,
And lower vibrational negativity to reject.

She had to learn to recognize,
She had to learn to face,
She had to align with her power,
Through her love and her truth and her grace.

She had to stand in her own strength,
But she had to let her compassion shine through,
She had to find balance as she gave to others,
And she had to allow love in for herself sometimes too.

We must refill the vessel,
The vessel which nurtures and feeds,
The vessel which heals and nourishes,
Let it not be overtaken by choking weeds.

The balance of love and releasing,
Releasing things which do not serve,
Rising above illusions to truth,
To maintain her radiant verve.

Don't poke too long at her armor,
Or one day you just might find and recover,
From the place you land in the mud at her feet,
Something you were meant there to discover.

She knows about compassion,
She knows a warrior's strength,
She is a giver of a type of love,
Which humanity loves to drink.

Janine Palmer (Silver Moon)

Your Truth Again

What do we do for humanity?
By healing ourselves always first?
It is then that we can be present to serve,
In the healing for which so many thirst.

So many don't even realize,
How they harm others from their unhealed pain,
Those lingering, weeping, bleeding wounds,
Which we bury instead of releasing, so they remain.

The wounds which silently scream for release,
The wounds which are triggered by so many things,
And so we create more pain and learn,
By what our thoughts and actions bring.

And we justify it by perspective,
It isn't really right or wrong,
It's one side of a perspective or an experience,
A different way to sing a song.

Until we learn to face the pain,
From the thing which created the wound,
Until we acknowledge it and heal it with forgiveness,
It will hold us hostage behind the moon.

We cannot see the true light,
While hiding behind the pain,
We miss so many beautiful opportunities,
And treasures we would gain.

What wounds will hold you hostage?
What if you face the pain and win?
Then you can rise out of illusion's grave,
To reunite with your truth again.

Janine Palmer (Silver Moon)

Quill

He wrote from his heart what it yearned for,
He wrote form his soul what it needed,
He wrote for his healing and manifestation,
It was a form of spiritual bleeding.

His quill was a magical tool,
It was an item of very great power,
Because the power of him came through,
As his spirit continued to flower.

A record of fantastic blossoming,
Was created by his weaving of words,
The thoughts and wisdom woven there,
With pen and paper now read and heard.

To share the written word,
Heart and soul on paper stored,
To be so open and vulnerable,
Is like the power and strength of a sword.

The beauty and humility,
The depth of a being laid bare,
Trickled out form the heart and soul,
To lay before you there.

A glimpse into another world,
To a dimension of somewhere so deep,
And the wisdom shared with compassion,
Is something you'll always keep.

Janine Palmer (Silver Moon)

Inner Planes

Sometimes she would access within,
Inner planes of wisdom's well,
She would access the love of her Sacred Heart,
Where God would always dwell.

To access the love of the Creator,
A beautiful endeavor indeed,
To reconnect with our true home,
Anytime we want to be free.

We are not stuck in this dimension,
But so many do not know,
They suffer due to illusion,
Which can affect the spirit's glow.

We won't find completion of ourselves,
In or through any other being,
They might reflect our beauty back to us,
Or aspects which need some healing.

We have everything within ourselves,
Which we could ever need,
Only we can show ourselves,
The truth we are not seeing.

Others might shine a light for us,
Through sharing love or pain,
But it's up to us to decide,
What wisdom from it we gain.

First should come acknowledgment,
Then surrender again to stand,
To send ourselves love from the highest,
To Source, The All, I AM.

Janine Palmer (Silver Moon)

Quiet Defiance

There's a quiet defiance about her,
One wonders from whence it came,
It often comes from emotional pain,
Being guarded against their blame.

The defiance is a type of strength,
The defiance is a type of reaction,
It might be armor set up somehow,
To protect her from rejection.

Defiance might be quiet aggression,
From things unspoken, from not feeling heard,
Maybe she didn't have the confidence to speak out,
Maybe she was not in touch with her words.

The defiance is an attempt at strength,
Which hasn't fully been exercised,
The defiance is a mask she wears,
Like any other disguise.

Janine Palmer (Silver Moon)

healing Flame

The healing flame was her essence,
The fire from which she was created,
She shared God's love and compassion,
She had experienced both love and hate.

Some did not recognize her light,
Some were jealous and didn't know why,
Some weren't ready to let go of their pain,
So in some inner tomb it would lie.

But eventually that pain must be released,
Else it will spew out in an unpleasant display,
It might harm the bearer or others,
When it burns them to ash it will show them the way.

The pain which eats people alive,
The pain which so consumes,
The unhealed wounds they will not face,
Creates a festering, noxious tomb.

Some aren't ready to hear God's messenger,
They are much too judgmental by far,
They would judge the messengers by its garment,
Not recognizing love from afar.

Some aren't open enough to continue to learn,
They think they have all the answers and the tools,
So they stay stuck at that part of their journeys,
But others might say they are fools.

The lower self and the higher,
The illusion and flame of the soul,
We all carry a healing flame within us,
Sometimes others just help it to grow.

We cannot ascend from the suffering here,
From a place of judgment so holier than thou,
We will be left behind again to be planted,
And the messengers are the plows.

Her healing flame will be recognized,
By those who are ready on their path,
To let go of their false ideologies,
To remove now darkness's gaff.

Those who rise well above,
Mindsets of needing to defend,
So many things they think they believe,
In order for their souls now to mend.

The healing flame is compassion,
The healing flame is love undescribed,
The healing flame is in you and me,
And when we recognize it is when we will thrive.

Don't persecute the messenger,
Who was sent by God with love,
Whether the messenger is dressed as raven,
Or whether it's dressed as a dove.

Janine Palmer (Silver Moon)

Quiet Wisdom

She listens to her inner self,
To the knowing which prevails,
The spirit dancing true and high,
Guiding her through breezes and gales.

She carries a quiet wisdom,
She wears it like a cloak,
Revealed to those awakening
Where cords were cut or broke.

Her wisdom like a compass,
Pointing to deeper truths,
Some might see the compassion which fuels her,
Some might think she is aloof.

Those who so engage her,
Gain a teacher and a friend,
Because what she shares is God's love,
Ongoing outwardly without end.

Love and gratitude create divine flow,
Returned to Source though us here,
Sacred tools and knowledge flow,
Through faith and trust, not fear.

Her quiet wisdom is a knowing,
Shared with her through guides,
Her world changed here for the better,
When no longer did she hide.

Our light here shouldn't be hidden,
Our light here is meant to be shared,
For the blessings which will flow ongoing,
When our compassion is purely bared.

Janine Palmer (Silver Moon)

Our Sacred Lands

Sacred lands are everywhere,
For those with eyes to see,
Sacred lands belong to no one,
They are part of you and me.

Sacred lands of the physical realm,
Sacred lands of our divine being,
Sacred lands of other dimensions,
Which so many are not seeing.

When we honor something,
We honor ourselves in return,
When we try to own or control,
Falsehoods will need to be burned.

Sacred fires are burning,
For us to so release,
Any pain or false thing we carry,
To rise above created grief.

Whether the pain is our ancestor's,
Or whether the pain is ours,
Some form of wisdom always comes,
Through the making of our scars.

Our scars do not define us,
They reflect some things quite great,
They testify to our strength and healing,
Where we learned through different gates.

Janine Palmer (Silver Moon)

Mirror, Mirror

Mighty

She is small but she is mighty,
Could it be the power of her love?
Or could it be the hidden magic?
She carries from the raven and the dove?

There are some who sense it,
Some who don't know what it is,
There are some who can see it, then and now,
And the compassion from which she gives.

There is a mightiness of character,
She brought in from heaven when she came,
Some are afraid of the power of it,
Others see glimpses of warriors from previous games.

Some can see the priestess,
Some can see the queen,
Some know the angel,
Some know of the witch in between.

Some recognize her goddess energy,
Some recognize the mother energy she shares,
Some recognize the flame of her compassion,
The passion which fuels what she dares.

A messenger and a healer,
An empress of the people with love,
A companion of the raven,
Here in service of the dove.

The light and shadow in combination,
From other dimensions a magic blend,
In balance and mysterious grace,
A star being here to help them ascend.

Those who recognize her familiar soul,
Those with open ears to hear the divine call,
Those who are open to healing their wounds,
Those who are ready to tear down their walls.

To throw down their armor in power,
To open to divine love and grace,
And to honor with love their brother,
And be blessed by the smile on his face.

She is love descended to earth,
For those awakening to recognize,
Those who can see through the veil,
Past the illusions and fallacies and lies.

The Divine Masculine is her balance,
The other half of her love,
Just like the magical combination here with her,
Of the raven and the dove.

Janine Palmer (Silver Moon)

Mirror of the Vagabond

Perspectives shift like the weather,
As the storms blow in and out,
Whether we stand or walk away,
While others scream and shout.

And what about the harmful effects,
From the pain of others which they hurl like darts?
Sending shards of their unhealed wounds toward others,
Venomous toxic projectiles, right into our hearts.

Sometimes when we try to help another,
Their burdens we might unknowingly take on,
Then they might begin to resent us in some manner,
And throw mud at the mirror of the vagabond.

And when traumatic things do happen,
When they shift us from places we are trapped,
They change our perspective in some needed way,
To help get us back on track.

We have to walk in awareness,
We should take stock of what we've learned,
We should shed our burdens which no longer serve,
Into the sacred fires to burn.

Janine Palmer (Silver Moon)

Sacred Shamanic Whispers

Our Own Spark

When someone holds something against you,
They also hold it against themselves,
And that is when we need to recognize,
We might need to walk away from that hell.

Sometimes a person holds things against you,
Things they use to judge,
Things they can't let go of to heal,
And from their position they won't budge.

That is a big flashing warning sign,
If you value yourself, to walk away,
There are others who will be grateful to accept you,
And not put road blocks in the way.

The unhealed things of this world,
Are the things many of us call 'dark',
Because they dim the glow of our soul,
To the degree that we don't recognize our own spark.

They bring things up to try to drag us down,
But they are things which need to be healed,
And so often the lid of the coffin,
Of a once beneficial connection is sealed.

Not that we don't still hold love,
Because of course our hearts still do;
There just comes a time that we choose no longer to swim,
In the harmful effects of others unhealed stew.

We all have things to heal,
But do we use them against a brother?
That is our choice which directs our path,
To things we are meant to discover.

Janine Palmer (Silver Moon)

God's Creatures

We must have so much care and compassion,
For so many beings here on this plane,
For we know not the pain that they carry,
We should never inflict any pain.

We must never abuse any of God's creatures,
We must carry an awareness that if we do,
That we will one day experience exactly what we inflict,
We will feel the results of the good or bad we do.

Any creature here on this earth,
Might be an angel here in disguise,
We are tested when we don't know it,
Does our behavior create happiness now or cries?

When you hear anyone cry out,
From any suffering you might create,
Consider yourself warned here now,
At some point you will enter that gate.

Janine Palmer (Silver Moon)

Observe

What is life trying to teach you?
What does it want you to observe?
What is your gift and purpose here?
And how are you meant to serve?

In what way can you serve humanity?
In what way can you endeavor to give back?
What can you do to maintain balance?
The place where there is no lack.

How does love flow out from your heart?
How do you share it with those in need?
How do you ask for what you want?
How do you heal the things which bleed?

What language do you speak to yourself?
What do mirrors reflect back to you?
Be careful what you say to others,
Since we're all connected and it comes back through.

Janine Palmer (Silver Moon)

Down Times

It's through ups and downs in Earth school,
During the down times we experience in life,
That we come to know our true friends,
By their healing hands or their knives.

When we experience hardships,
Sometimes help comes from others we might need,
And it's during these times we see behind the masks,
To whether they will support us or leave us to bleed.

To kick a brother when he is down,
Is very greatly frowned upon,
Revealing issues buried in a person,
Who appear to be a lower vibrational pawn.

To withdraw a hand instead of extending it,
Is to show how God does or doesn't work through you,
It's a form of dishonor to the highest,
When you won't allow it to come through.

It might be time to look in the mirror,
Especially if you think you know grace,
Because it might be possible you don't see it too clearly,
Through the mask upon your face.

But similarly there are also times,
When we have to step back let someone walk their path,
Even though they are creating destruction,
From something which they lack.

Janine Palmer (Silver Moon)

Beauty of the Creator in All

Find the balance within your beauty,
Beauty known or unknown on so many levels,
But we might have to rise above,
The illusions of so many devils.

There is beauty in every being,
Even when they try to hide it away,
Even when they don't see it in themselves,
Because of falsehoods they have not yet slayed.

Falsehoods which cloud their true vision,
Falsehoods which they 'believe',
Falsehoods which block their forward movement,
And the things they could achieve.

When they can rise out of that fog,
Past the illusion, beyond the veil,
They might begin to recognize their own beauty,
The beauty of the Creator which will always prevail.

The beauty they see in others,
Is a reflection of themselves,
But many don't recognize it as such,
Because in their truth they don't yet dwell.

Some of us exist in false perception,
Of someone else's perceived or programmed truth,
And many of these are the judgmental ones,
Who shun and remain separate and aloof.

Look deeply through an internal mirror,
To see the aspects of God within,
Above and beyond any fear or guilt,
And beyond the illusion of sin.

Above any vengeful or wrathful god,
To remember the high God of love,
Not any lower jealous god,
Who feeds off of sacrifice and blood.

Sadly it seems many people have these confused,
Because of darkness's programming parade,
Because they program mankind to feel unworthy,
To forget from whom they were made.

What is this dark force which feeds,
Off of the suffering mankind has made?
Why do they perpetuate through misunderstanding,
For mankind to continually fall on its blade?

No being of the high God,
Is unworthy in any way,
How could that possibly be?
Our illusions we must slay.

To keep mankind in any illusion,
Of being unworthy is keep him trapped,
And thus to keep him in control,
In guilt and fear and lack.

The beauty of the Creator,
Is the compassionate flame within,
The flame of love we can't explain,
But when we find it our life begins.

Janine Palmer (Silver Moon)

Boomerang Words & Deeds

The words which you spew forth,
Formed from mouths or fingertips,
From the thoughts of the monkey mind,
Come back to you as gifts.

Whatever type of energy,
You spew out into the world,
Will work its way right back to you,
Are you listening, boys and girls?

Do you share the love of God?
Through yourself upon this earth?
Or do you share your toxic waste?
Before you find re-birth?

Oh do be careful what you say,
Be careful what energy you share,
As you will have to experience that too,
Whether painful, foul or fair.

The nasties which seem to fester in us,
Which we know not how to release,
Often come out to harm our loved ones,
From the forgotten bowels of our keep.

Make sure to keep a tidy home,
Make sure you clean the floors,
Or else the dirt and clutter might build up,
Blocking entrance and exit doors.

Janine Palmer (Silver Moon)

Shedding Skins & Shells

No Rights to Slavery

The governments of some countries here,
Are ruled by darkness in disguise,
It goes way beyond any 'white man',
And all different kinds of tribes.

Darkness can so infiltrate,
Any color of skin,
Keeping man stuck like a pawn,
And so the light does not get in.

So many people want to focus,
Only now upon one thing,
But they are not seeing the bigger picture here,
And the wisdom it would bring.

Take for example slavery,
Not only suffered by any one race,
And way before Africa started doing it,
Jews and Christians were also slaves.

And let us really not forget,
That some cultures were selling their own,
Yet we try to blame it on the other color,
And for that we must atone.

So many cultures throughout time here,
Have suffered from this control and greed,
The Greeks, the Moors, the Irish,
And darkness does it feed.

So many are slaves to religions,
To somebody else's ideas about things,
To misinterpretation and mistranslation,
And the damage that it brings.

Some women have been slaves to men,
We are slaves to our thoughts about things,
We are slaves to cultural ideologies and programming,
Until we break out of the shell, to our purpose which sings.

If we choose to remain in the role of victim,
And keep our ancestor's pain alive,
Then we and they can't move forward,
To the evolvement toward which we strive.

Many tribes of many cultures,
Were slaves thousands of years before,
Because some rulers had no regard for their brethren,
And the rulers became darkness's whore.

Darkness would have us be so cruel,
Using the reason of the color of someone's skin,
And when we get caught up in that trap,
Our true purpose cannot begin.

Keeping us from moving forward,
Has long been the plan here on this earth,
But that is rapidly changing now,
As so many awaken to their rebirth.

The dark deeds on this planet,
Go far beyond what we can see,
And until we let go of the old pain,
Darkness will have control over you and me.

The slaves of thousands of years ago,
May not have had much of a voice,
Many did not even know how to write,
So acknowledgement is by our choice.

Those who came after them and their relatives,
Are being a voice here for it now,
The key is to disengage from the darkness of it,
But only love can show us how.

No one culture has rights to stay stuck in slavery,
Because over the millennia so many have been affected,
And when we don't acknowledge them all,
We stay stuck where we need redirection.

Be the love your ancestor's needed then,
Be the love you are here now,
Rise above the clutches of darkness,
To which you no longer need to bow.

To create something good here now,
From something bad before,
Propels us forward on our path,
Through new ascension doors.

Janine Palmer (Silver Moon)

The Burden

His armor became too heavy,
His trust issues created a gate,
Which was locked and he had forgotten the key,
Trapped in illusion, fear and hate.

So many of us walk our path,
Dragging our burdens behind,
Even though we might partially see through the mists,
Parts of us might still be spiritually blind.

He seemed to resist blessings which were sent to him,
As he was hiding behind his pain,
And his inability to communicate,
Prevented things he would otherwise gain.

The walls he'd built around himself,
Made it very hard to see,
They prevented the entrance of good things,
And because of them he was not free.

He seemed afraid to step out,
Onto a mysterious path unknown,
Because previous hurtful situations,
Needed acknowledgment to atone.

He didn't mean to hurt them,
Those he loved whom he pushed away,
But until he could tear down his walls,
His armor would block the light of day.

The key is buried in him,
Under all that old pain he can't seem to release,
Layers and layers of illusions,
Which chain him to his grief.

Janine Palmer (Silver Moon)

Beckoning Intent

When intention becomes fruition,
It continues to swirl and move,
And depending on how it's cared for,
Will it fly or stay stuck in grooves?

When we beckon with intention,
And creation moves and glows,
It depends on whether it's nurtured,
Whether it withers or whether it grows,

What do we create by our behavior here?
Does it nurture or does it maim?
Does it come from our higher self from love,
Or from the lower self of wrath and blame?

When someone becomes a whipping boy,
They are driven well away,
Until one day an offender might look back,
And wonder why they didn't stay.

If we cannot take responsibility,
For the things which we create,
We might stumble on in confusion,
Do we feed love or do we feed hate?

They say the road to hell is paved,
With good intentions all the way,
We have to shed and release our old skins,
To meet the freshness of a new day.

And if we cannot find a way,
To be kind to our sisters and brothers,
It is ourselves we end up choking,
And our own happiness which we smother.

Beckon from your higher self,
Beckon what you would like to receive,
And make sure you give the same to others,
Or of your own truth you will be a thief.

Be careful what you conjure up,
That it's not a poisonous, toxic stew,
Because what you fling at others,
In some way comes back to you.

Janine Palmer (Silver Moon)

Destruction

Sometimes destruction is necessary,
To tear away the old shells,
To shed old skins to reveal the new,
To free ourselves from hell.

Like a type of shamanic dismemberment,
Like dying to the old for the new,
For the purpose of rebirth and rising above,
As new wisdom now whispers through.

Destroying the old we learned from,
Destroying what serves us no more,
To shed our burdens so we are small enough,
To fit through mysterious new doors.

Destroying illusions like heavy capes,
Which hang round us wearing masks of belief,
Illusions through gross misperceptions,
Of our happiness it becomes a thief.

Thinking and believing falsehoods,
Things are not always what they appear,
But we react in error creating pain,
Creating lack and walls and fear.

So allow the destruction to happen,
Allow the emotions to flow through,
Don't let them get stuck to be carried around,
As great burdens to be shouldered by you.

Shed the old skins and broken shells,
Lighten the loads you carry,
You can start by removing and releasing,
Anything you tend to bury.

Your temple is not a graveyard,
To house old illusions of pain,
Clear the cobwebs from your temple,
Let in the wind and the rain.

The wind of spirit which dances,
In and out of the truth and illusion you see,
And rain like the tears you must let flow,
If you want again to be free.

Allow yourself to be cleansed,
But the destruction you thought you feared,
To make room for new blessings to come,
After your sacred house is cleared.

Janine Palmer (Silver Moon)

The Path

No one can battle your demons for you,
They are things you must release,
Because of your energy and your power,
They become unrecognized debilitating thieves.

We weaken our energy by carrying burdens,
We weaken ourselves by carrying pain,
We become weak when we don't release old grief,
And unnecessary sadness do we gain.

We must remove the rubbish,
We must find the tools to take our power back,
We must rise above the ashes of what we burn,
To move toward abundance and out of lack.

When we project our issues,
Onto anyone else along our path,
We sometimes negatively affect their energy,
And karma is a circulating kind of map.

Take responsibility for your energy,
Even if you don't yet know how,
When you take a step out onto the path,
The path will open to show you now.

To be able to identify the demon(s),
To be able to identify the patterns,
To identify the habits which do not serve,
So you can repair your sails which are tattered.

Your savior is yourself,
With the help of masters and guides,
And when you shine your light on your demons,
There is nowhere for them now to hide.

Send yourself the most beautiful love,
From divinity your home on high,
And share it with everyone you meet,
For collective healing now by and by.

Janine Palmer (Silver Moon)

The Love

The love of the Creator,
Through so many beings flows,
Some will see it and honor it,
For others too bright is the glow.

Some will recognize the gifts to be shared,
And accept it with gratitude and grace,
Others will try to spit on it,
But it might splash back in their face.

What we do comes back to us,
Whether its love or whether its hate,
We create our reality with our thoughts you know,
Do you create a cell or do you create a gate?

Do you allow love to flow through you?
Do you pick and choose due to pain?
Do you take the knowledge from experience?
Do you heal or do you maim?

Do you release what no longer serves you?
Do you fling arrows or darts or spears?
And are you fueled by venom you won't release?
By holding onto pain and doubt and fear?

Invite your higher self to assist you,
To disconnect from any old pain,
To make room for the new blessings trying to come to you,
And then healing you will gain.

Janine Palmer (Silver Moon)

Tangled Threads

Our connections here are many,
Some give, some test, some take,
Some create joy, some create pain,
All for experience's sake.

Sometimes the threads get tangled,
Sometimes they must be severed,
Some are pure and true,
Some are cheeky and clever.

When things are in knots or tangled,
We must be patient and be still,
We must thoughtfully work the knots loose,
Exercising respect by our free will.

Sometimes things seem to get mixed up,
Between our heart and our mind,
Sometimes we wear our blinders,
And meet ignorance in kind.

But tangles can be worked through,
Do we comb through or do we cut them?
Do we hide away in fear?
Or do we let new rays of light in?

The wound is where the light enters us,
We are cracked open in so many ways,
And what we find when we are on our knees,
Are tools to guide us through the maze.

Our individual journeys,
And the things which we will find,
When we open to our truth within,
Will loosen falsehoods and unbind.

When we cut away the old threads,
Of things which no longer serve,
We become free to accept new threads of love,
Which nurture and heal our verve.

Janine Palmer (Silver Moon)

False hell

She battled through the riff raff,
She climbed the mountains tall,
She bandaged up her bruises,
Every time she took a fall.

She shared the energy of her compassion,
Which came from the deepest love divine,
She did her best from the remembered knowledge,
Trudging through the muck of the swine.

Sometimes when she would wash the filth away,
In some tranquil cleansing pond,
Her reflection was something she often didn't recognize,
Because there were times she had come undone.

Sometimes she resembled a haggard warrior,
Sometimes she was a mother of love very deep,
Sometimes she was wife and mother,
And sometimes they didn't recognize her and left her to weep.

But the strength she ever needed,
Could always be found within herself,
And in nature always replenishing,
She tore away and burned any remnants of false hell.

Janine Palmer (Silver Moon)

Countless Pieces

Countless pieces of many things,
Coming and going and breaking,
Countless blessings flowing to us,
In gratitude for the taking.

Pieces of hearts so broken,
Floating around us in disarray,
Until we put them back in place,
While our demons we slay.

Our demons don't need to be scary,
They test us while we are here,
They challenge us to find the pieces of strength,
From all the times we have visited here.

Whatever that means to a being,
Not linear, this spiraling time,
As we recognize our divine connections,
To the collective and the vine.

Call back the pieces of your broken heart,
Call back the pieces of your soul,
It's time to put them back in the rightful places,
To heal their radiant glow.

Janine Palmer (Silver Moon)

Born from the Wreckage

Bursting forth from a place of hardship,
Whether heartache, illusion or change,
When things are shifted from being shaken,
Parts of our reality are so rearranged.

What things are born from the wreckage?
What parts rise when other parts fall?
What parts inspire something in you?
What would happen if you took down your walls?

Things are born from destruction,
We have to sift through the wreckage and the ash,
Wounds don't really heal,
Until we stitch up the gash.

But before we close the wound,
We need to clean it out,
If we stitch it up with debris inside it,
The pain will make us shout.

We need to remove from our temple,
Anything not sacred to our soul,
For the greater good of our being,
For the spirit and the heart to glow.

What things have been buried from the wreckage?
The things in life which have burned,
The things which seem like failure or loss,
But there is always wisdom earned.

Is self-love ever present,
In the pure well of your heart?
A type of love you can share with humanity,
Because that's where healing starts.

Janine Palmer (Silver Moon)

Proud and Lonely

Is it pride which makes us push away,
The love we really need?
Is it pride or fear or hiding,
Which causes us to make others bleed?

Is standing our ground in resistance,
Worth the murder of love once great?
Is identification with victim mentality,
A secret key to Hell's dark gate?

To be too proud to apologize,
Too proud to admit any fault,
To live in a void of false self-righteousness,
Is to put part of oneself in a vault.

Lonely are those who can't face themselves,
Lonely are those who believe lies,
Lonely are those mired in wounds and fear,
Who are controlled by the disguise.

Trying to keep things away for protection,
Keeps love away from your door,
Eventually we might find ourselves,
Flat on the threshing room floor.

Where we will be invited,
To sort through what to release,
To let go of what doesn't serve us,
Like guilt and shame and fear and grief.

Janine Palmer (Silver Moon)

Shedding Skins

Diving into the clear pond,
Only for a revitalizing swim,
To enter a sacred place,
To recharge to feel whole again.

Down so deep she was taken,
Shedding all of her skin,
Until she was only the rawness of herself,
For healing to begin.

In stillness she waded in the darkness,
To reflect and face her fear,
To allow the knots to unravel,
To sever, to release, to clear.

She had shed her skin like the serpent,
The layers of illusion's stories,
The remnants of unhealed pain,
And doubt and fear and worries.

Now just the rawest essence,
Of her there in the deep,
In the darkened realm of healing,
Where glimpses of wisdom seep.

Shown to her through the light of her soul,
Remembered through her heart and her mind,
To help her traverse the path of amnesia,
To cut the ties which bind.

To unplug from things which kept her stuck,
To unplug from programs foul,
To set the wolf within her free,
At her sacred moon to howl.

With answers received, and guidance,
Back to the top she floated more healed,
To return more restored and stronger,
Between what is and isn't real.

The things which seem to hurt us,
Are not as real as they seem,
In realms we enter with ancestors and guides,
Are where truth and wisdom is gleaned.

Sacred realms where angels dance,
Where divine fires forge our light,
Until we descend into the realm of unknowing,
Forgetting as we do our magnificent birthright.

And so we are challenged with many things,
Through tests we pass and fail,
But we discover are we always worthy,
When we shatter illusion's nails.

She had to look deeply into her depths,
To find what still held her back,
To find the ties which kept her stuck,
In the illusion of doubt and fear and lack.

Through different grueling experiences,
She found her perspectives had now changed,
Thank the gods for shining their light,
Into the fog of the preordained.

Janine Palmer (Silver Moon)

Initiations & Battle Scars

Experiences as Tools

The experiences she has had here,
Have been lessons for valuable things learned,
And so she shares what was gained with others,
Received by some with gratefulness or by others spurned.

Some receive the pearls of wisdom,
From her words written from love and grace,
Some would rather throw tar from their inner venom,
As the mask slips away to reveal another face.

The ugliness present from their old pain,
Revealing itself from some hellish cell,
Preferring to find fault and point a finger in blame,
Than to stand in their power ringing freedom's bell.

To hold things against another,
Is to hold things against thyself,
They seem very unaware of untapped resources,
Hidden within themselves.

How in the world will they learn to let go?
How will they learn to take their power back?
As they crawl through the tar of the own jealous hatred,
Through the blood spilled from their vicious attacks.

Crawling through the tar of life,
From the blood they continue to spill,
Somehow they cannot live with themselves,
Because of their unreleased screams so shrill.

Allow the screams to be released,
Use that energy for fuel,
Create something good from what appeared to be bad,
Use your experiences as tools.

Janine Palmer (Silver Moon)

War or Peace

She overheard a conversation,
Something discussed so long ago,
From lessons learned through life experiences,
Wisdom for the flow.

If you wanted peace,
Why did you start the war?
How did jealousies and perspective,
Get the upper hand and slam the door?

Why do things get blown out or proportion?
We focus on something so much it becomes power,
Things which aren't full truth become destructive,
Ripping the petals off of a once beautiful flower.

The thing you made such a big deal of,
You let bother you to the core,
Exploding in destructive sabotage,
And something once loved is now no more.

Destroyed by the illusion,
Sabotaged by ego's actions,
Finding fault where there should be love,
Can't seem to get any satisfaction.

Choose your battles wisely,
Before you find yourself at an empty gate,
Due to ego's love of being offended,
By feeding the programs of hate.

Janine Palmer (Silver Moon)

Blood Stains

What was this hell she walked through?
What was this hell on earth?
Was it simply part of the learning journey?
Part of the initiations of rebirth?

She emerged from a very hellish place,
Which seemed to be suffering without end,
There were blood stains splattered all over her gown,
And new wounds which needed to mend.

She was sent here for this purpose,
But there was so much she did not remember,
And through the gauntlet of the mystery here,
There was destruction through ash and cinder.

When she emerged from the dark cave,
She noticed how her gown dragged heavily upon the ground,
Mud and tar and blood round the hem,
Remnants of the despair she had found.

The filth they threw at her in anguish,
Red and black marred her garment and wore her down,
But the faeries were there to assist her,
To help her find a smile instead of a frown.

They were waiting for her to appear there,
And they quickly cut away the blood and tar from the hem,
They took her to a soothing bath,
And left her there to swim.

There she shed a hundred tears,
For all the tortured souls she had encountered,
They reminded her of her own ascension,
And of the scale of things she'd surmounted.

She washed away her own blood,
And she also washed away theirs,
Because she didn't need to carry any of that pain,
Which serves not any of the heirs.

She had to find her deepest strength,
Through this initiation she had passed so well,
By walking through the fiery gauntlet,
Of the venom spewing from human hell.

It came from sources unexpected,
It came from those she called friends,
It came from the dark energy of their demons,
Which were unreleased so the suffering didn't end.

Her blood which was spilled there on her gown,
Which represented her physical DNA,
But possibly more important than that,
Is her spiritual DNA which guides her way.

She saw her reflection in a pool,
And there appeared something before unseen,
She saw an image behind herself,
Of the beauty of her own wings.

Janine Palmer (Silver Moon)

Not My Business

I'm learning along my journey,
It matters not what other people think,
We each create our own reality,
From the effects of the thoughts we drink.

I've lost connections with people,
Who I thought were my closest friends,
But life has lessons it wants me to learn,
As I navigate its twists and bends.

People might hold things against you,
In ways that are not even true,
There might be fears, insecurities and jealousies,
Which present to be used against you.

People often attack what they don't understand,
They so often act out from their unhealed pain,
But what they don't realize until after the fact,
Is that they push away the people they maim.

If we don't take responsibility to heal,
If we don't learn how to release,
Then the cost might be our own happiness,
Our patterns and habits are thieves.

I've learned that when people say unkind things about me,
When they tell or believe falsehoods which aren't true,
That is an invitation to the infinite power in me,
For strength and healing now to come through.

I must be very aware, however,
To look for the lessons these things are trying to teach,
To become aware of things in me which need healing,
And closer to divine love do I reach.

I am learning I have to let go of,
People's unkind thoughts about me in any way,
It's not my business what they choose to hold,
It's my business to disconnect from things which would slay.

Just because someone spreads or believes,
A venomous lie or any twisted truth incomplete,
For my own acceptance and forward movement,
I don't need to be in defense or compete.

If we function from true compassion,
With no ill will against anyone,
Then it is enough to walk in our truth,
Even if others might shun.

I'm thankful for what many friends have taught me,
Even if it's that things are not what they seem,
Everything is always unfolding,
As we trudge through illusion and the dream.

Sometimes there are nightmares,
But they don't have to be where we exist,
We cannot fix or exist in,
Others unhealed wounds which resist.

I can send love to dysfunctional situations,
As I warrior up and walk away,
Toward the next lesson a little bit wiser,
Not caring or carrying what they might say.

Janine Palmer (Silver Moon)

The Plow

The Mystery is in your neighbor,
The Mystery is in you,
What makes either of you tick?
What unfolds to bring you clues?

What bits and pieces are revealed?
At any given time here and now,
How do things unfold and direct you?
Do you push or pull the plow?

We see things from certain perspectives,
We have a limited understanding at best,
We respond or react accordingly,
These things are always a test.

We can pull the plow without question for others,
Or we can push it where we want it to go,
We can be the captain of our own ship,
Or be a passenger of life, you know.

Try to view things from different angles,
And from that you will always learn more,
You might be given more opportunities,
To venture through more doors.

Be open to the wonder of the Mystery,
And for whatever you learn there is much more,
So much more to learn than you could ever fathom,
So many adventures for you to explore.

Bravery is an aspect of the warrior,
So are patience and compassion in place,
So is strength gained through initiations,
Through the challenging things we all face.

Janine Palmer (Silver Moon)

Unknown/Unseen

What so many don't really understand,
Is that each being agrees to have experiences here,
For what it will teach them or those they love,
Even through loss and pain and things which aren't clear.

Some might only agree to be here,
For a limited amount of time,
And when they leave us we are challenged to grow,
But we suffer when we're spiritually blind.

If we stay too focused,
On loss and grief and pain,
We might hinder the path of the one we lost,
Their soul's forward movement we might just restrain.

When we focus too long on our own pain,
And don't learn to release the grief,
We hold them and ourselves as spiritual hostages,
And of our own happiness we are a thief.

We never lose the soul connections we have,
And when we step out of suffering we can feel,
The presence of their spirits as they visit us in dreams,
While they help our hearts to heal.

Maybe they agreed to come here,
And then leave for us to learn,
To become stronger and to rise above illusion,
And what does not serve us we should burn.

They don't want to see us suffer,
Everything experienced is by some type of choice,
Whether in spirit before we came here,
In this free will zone, or pre-agreement's voice.

Most of us do not remember our purpose here,
Or the sacred contracts we made,
With so many souls for evolvement,
Upon this earth school stage.

So many initiations and tests here,
So many things which rise and fall,
To test us to become aware of the illusions,
Before we reconnect with the All.

There are reasons people leave us,
In the various ways they do,
No one is meant to remain here,
This realm is only a school.

Keep this pearl of wisdom,
That things are not what they seem,
And all those we love are safe in love,
We are living here in a dream.

You can learn to tune in to them,
You can learn to reconnect,
They are always connected to us,
In our hearts where their love reflects.

The mind does not understand,
But the heart it always will,
Allow your angels to help you,
To release, to flow, to heal.

But while we are here we must learn,
To regain our warrior strength once again,
To rise above sadness, resentment and pain,
To be able to allow their presence back in.

And when you reunite with them,
On a level of love much higher than this,
You will smile in recognition and understanding,
Back home in a state of divine bliss.

Janine Palmer (Silver Moon)

Dastardly Deeds

The dastardly deeds you perpetrate,
You store in a karmic belt around your waist,
Everything you do good or bad,
At some point you will know and taste.

Whatever it is that you reap,
Of course comes from what you sow,
Whether you are planting flowers or weeds,
What energy through you will flow?

Will your energetic vibration rise?
And with compassion will you create?
Or will it stay in the lower realms,
Of anger, resentment and hate?

Will you identify with the victim?
Will sadness rule the day?
Will you live in your past or in fear of the future?
Or will you rise out of that spiritual grave?

You will graduate from initiations?
As you come back in tune with the truth of yourself?
As you rise above ego and illusion,
To where the divinity in you always dwells.

But when you commit dastardly deeds,
Against yourself or any other,
You keep yourself chained away from your higher self,
And your happiness do you smother.

Find the tools within yourself,
To sever the unwanted ties,
To take your magnificent power back now,
From the falsehoods, illusions and lies.

Janine Palmer (Silver Moon)

Echoes

Energy echoes through eternity,
Through light and dark around,
Through beings, worlds and dimensions,
Through ancestors, memories and sound.

Experiences of the soul,
Treasures of wisdom gained,
Applied, passed down and hidden,
Through initiations sustained.

Echoes of love always dancing,
In and out of time then and now,
Always with us known and unknown,
As we ride on destiny's plow.

Sacred agreements made in spirit,
Choices by free will made,
As we cut through illusion's veil,
With the sacred fire of our own blade.

Realities here so created,
By choices and decisions here,
Through the curious mists of illusion,
And usually not very clear.

So steered by our intuition,
And steered by love so divine,
As we begin to remember our magnificence,
Through our connectedness to the vine.

Janine Palmer (Silver Moon)

Cave of Initiation

On this journey like many others,
And every time she must rise,
Part of her came back here,
Garbed in some disguise.

A high priestess beginning to remember,
Because she was open to being shown,
She opened her self to remember,
Wisdom already known.

In the cave of initiation,
As challenges are faced and passed,
As she learns to detach from the illusion of the pain,
And from the falsehoods which would hold her back.

To recognize incomplete beliefs,
Which are swirling all around,
Which would try to shackle her firmly,
And hold her to the ground.

But by recognizing their falseness,
It takes their power away,
And she can rise up to do God's work,
Through her truth and light and way.

Many will recognize her spirit,
And also there are those who will not,
Because many stumble along, asleep,
Hijacked by the beliefs they've bought.

The priests and priestesses of the orders,
Who are here to help humanity rise,
Awakened ambassadors here for God,
Who have shed all earthly disguise.

The cave has tested them harshly,
They have passed initiations and tests,
And they are called to be of service,
And by their love we are so blessed.

Janine Palmer (Silver Moon)

Inner Battles

We all fight inner battles,
Of which others are unaware,
We all misperceive so many things,
Sometimes compassion seems so rare.

Is it so difficult to imagine,
Yourself in someone else's shoes?
And to have some empathy for another?
Ignorance is all you lose.

Sometimes someone will share with you,
Something about a burden they carry,
Or sometimes they keep it buried inside,
And of that ye should be wary.

Be wary of how it might come out,
One day when least expected,
Like a volcano erupting uncontrollably,
Toward you by something reflected.

The battles are few or many,
Experienced by all on this earth,
Part of the initiations of earth school,
Until we experience rebirth.

Send love to the battle weary,
Even if it is yourself,
And shine a light into the dark corners,
Where fear and ignorance dwell.

Janine Palmer (Silver Moon)

The hard Parts

It's the hard parts of the journey,
Which bring the greatest gifts,
Those seemingly horrible initiations,
Which bring about the greatest shifts.

It might be pain or anger,
Which forces a change for some relief,
It might be a change in perspective,
Which will move us out of grief.

But we must give our permission,
We must be open to heal and evolve,
We must stop holding things against ourselves,
We are not a problem to solve.

We must flow through life like a river,
We might trickle or we might rage,
We must move around hard obstacles,
To turn or write another page.

We will hopefully begin to discover,
The folly of holding things against another,
Because we unknowingly do to ourselves,
Whatever we do to our brother.

Janine Palmer (Silver Moon)

Enemies Rising (?)

Who or what is the enemy?
Humans disconnected from God...
Who stumble in their dark ignorance,
And upon others they often trod.

Disconnected from their higher selves,
And to their lower ego selves they cling,
As they crawl through initiation's gauntlets,
They try to take down those who sing.

Those who sing are beings,
Trying to remind those who suffer and sleep,
To remember now their divinity,
To disconnect from the illusions which make us weep.

So when someone appears to be an enemy,
Remember they have wounds unhealed,
Remember they might be disconnected and stuck in darkness,
No knowing what is real.

Life is full of illusion,
Pretending to be real,
And when we allow ourselves to be misled,
Our peace it just might steal.

They might be disconnected from their compassion,
They might be stuck in unforgiveness's cell,
They might be crying out for help,
Ready to leave behind their hell.

But maybe they don't possess the tools,
Maybe they don't know how,
So when life knocks them to their knees,
They learn to take a bow.

When we can recognize this deeper truth,
When we can detach and take a step back,
And not take things so personally,
Because it's not about us, why they attack.

The enemy can be dark thought forms,
Habits and patterns we carry,
Or programs we run which control us,
From the old pain which we bury.

Buried pain and emotion,
Will work its way to the top,
Eventually spewing out like a volcano,
Breaking through walls and locks.

And when it does it's not pretty,
And when it does it might hurt,
But that is the beginning,
Of rising out of the ashes for rebirth.

When you make the necessary peace,
With your very own inner self,
By remembering where you come from,
You can walk out of any cell.

When you can learn to detach,
From being too entangled with the physical world,
You will no longer be an enemy to yourself,
Or to other boys or girls.

Janine Palmer (Silver Moon)

Judgment & Ego

Guidelines

What in the world is a belief system?
And how does it know if it's right?
If it was stripped of its ego…
Would it regain its unhindered sight?

And what about the individuals,
Who make up any particular group?
Are they there because they found their inner truth?
Not if they are jumping through hoops.

Belief systems and ideologies,
Can also be seen as idols to which we bow,
Our attachment to our preconceived ideas,
Are the obstacles blocking our plow.

Belief systems can be guidelines,
Which might contain truth in part,
But they cannot compare to the truth of Divinity,
Which exists within every man's heart.

Things we come across in this world,
Things we read or listen to in order to learn,
Might lead us to that inner truth,
But they're not our complete truth which ever burns.

Why do we cling to certain ideas?
When things outside of us might only point to the truth?
Like the finger pointing toward the moon,
It's unwise to believe anything outside of us, is in anyway absolute.

We are not sheep following along here,
Following along with the right or wrong crowd,
At some point some of us awaken,
To the call of our soul so loud.

We get caught in traps here due to fear,
We get stuck in things because we sleep,
It's only when we awaken, to our worthiness and divinity,
That we uncover great treasure, which is always ours to keep.

Remember that man often misinterprets things,
Remember that man makes mistakes,
Remember that man learns from experiences,
And is the power and the key to his own divine gate.

Janine Palmer (Silver Moon)

The Lower

We all have gifts and power,
But what if lower ego has its way?
What if in our disconnection from our higher self,
The innocent and the good we slay?

What if the shadow part of ourselves,
Is heavier than the part which is light?
What if there is a gross imbalance?
Where we feel the need to maim and fight?

Does that fuel a part of us?
Does it create positive things which come back?
From the harmful things we create?
From some part of ourselves in lack?

Can we recognize the patterns and behavior?
Can we recognize when we're being cruel?
Is it because something has control over us?
We should never be ego's great fool.

Ego serves us to a degree,
The ego tests us here,
But it should not have the upper hand,
Over how we treat or brothers and sisters so dear.

Every heart you injure,
Anywhere you cause pain or fear,
Are collections of things you will also get to experience,
So will you create smiling or will your create tears?

It's really very simple,
Just because we haven't been treated well,
Doesn't mean we need to do the same to someone else,
That just perpetrates the ongoing patterns of hell.

We know when we have risen here,
To a higher vibrational level,
When we create good from the bad,
Which frees us from our hell.

Transmutation is a magnificent force,
Transmuting negative things to light,
For the collective to rise in love,
Above the illusions of wrong and right.

Janine Palmer (Silver Moon)

Release

Some of what you can't stand in others,
Are triggers of unhealed things in yourself,
Perhaps things in need of acknowledgement and release,
To release ourselves from hell.

When things trigger us and we judge,
These are things in need of healing,
Because these are the patterns and habits,
And our happiness they are stealing.

To judge makes one feel superior,
And that is the a devious little lie,
Our task here is to rise above these tests,
Part of our ascension here by and by.

We can recognize in the behavior of others,
How we don't want to be,
And when we can observe and not react,
We have risen above it you see.

This is how we are strengthened,
Extreme reaction is how we give our power away,
The strength is to stand in our power,
In our own truth and light on our way.

Janine Palmer (Silver Moon)

Negativity

Do you feed off of negativity?
Or have you overcome that program you run?
Do you talk badly about others in your righteousness?
Is your first response to judge and to shun?

Do you easily feel offended?
Which is the ego's lower self at work,
Trying to shine a light on self-importance,
By the habits and patters we serve.

Do you ever reflect on something,
Which felt hurtful or did not resonate?
Which felt unfair or out of balance,
So your response was to retaliate?

And did you ever wonder,
If you really had all the facts?
Before you judged another and burned them at the ego's stake?
And when will you take your power back?

Did you ever turn the tables?
Did you ever create something good from the bad?
Have you ever create something positive from it?
Feeding happy instead of sad.

Do you hold things against another?
And do you realize you're really holding things against yourself?
Do you try to make other people feel bad,
From the cockpit of your cell?

Do you create negativity?
How heavy is your cross?
Who is really in charge of you?
Are your patterns really your boss?

Be very aware of patterns,
Those things which rule you now,
Don't keep going into programmed negativity,
To which you often bow.

Does it serve your higher purpose?
Are you aware that it binds?
When you trudge through the muck of negativity,
Do you think there's something you're supposed to find?

Does it serve you in a good way?
In any way does it keep you bound?
In recurring, conditioned, habitual responses,
Slithering along on the ground?

Do you know what it feels like to make a difference?
When you shed the negative cloak you wear?
When you break free of the patterns of negativity,
That false master you will no longer bear.

Perhaps one day you will notice,
How nasty the behavior is,
And perhaps like the phoenix you will rise from it,
More powerful in more positive bliss.

Maybe you will focus on the good,
In yourself and everyone else,
And thank the new wings for their part,
In lifting you out of your cell.

Janine Palmer (Spirit Silver Moon)

Self-Discovery or Ego?

Ego wears so many masks,
Many of which do not serve,
Many create blocks to growth,
And disrupt our energetic verve.

When we choose to be offended,
It might be an ego flare,
When we are too into ourselves in shallow ways,
We are likely in the ego's lair.

It's such a tricky challenge,
To find balance between humility and strength of self,
To be humble while supporting your own self-discovery,
As you dig deeper into your own well.

To discover beautiful things about yourself,
And to honor the bigger and better parts of who you are,
While still remaining humble and compassionate,
All the while healing from previous scars.

To rise out of any notions of feeling unworthy,
To embrace so many different parts of yourself,
Even if others don't fully accept you,
Because your individual journey is not where they dwell.

And it's trickier to accept the darker parts,
Of ourselves which others like to point out,
To try to knock us down or keep us down,
But that's what learning is all about.

People might try to beat you down,
Disapproving of your forward movement somehow,
When they know nothing of your pre-agreements,
But would rather judge and find fault with you here and now.

Their unhealed wounds might trigger you,
Or your unhealed wounds might trigger them,
And as long as that and defensive actions are occurring,
Then old patterns and habits continue as a ruling sin.

Sin means missing the point here,
Defensiveness is protection from pain,
And when we feel the need to defend ourselves,
From neither will either now gain.

When someone oversteps the boundaries,
Of honoring a person or not,
Things might be said which are harmful,
Our experiences are created by thought.

When we point the finger in blame,
And when we continue to find fault and error,
We often push away those we love,
While damaging things once cherished and fair.

And so many refuse to apologize,
They would rather hold onto their ideas of being right,
Which seems to be more important to them than the person they love,
Perpetrating the pushing of them out into the night.

The night of misunderstanding,
Miscommunication causing pain which destroys,
The hardships and battles between so many people,
Where love once reigned between girls and boys.

Janine Palmer (Silver Moon)

Unrecognized Angels

Sometimes trapped in this lower realm,
Of materialism and ego's lair,
Of wanting to be right and righteousness,
We trip on tests and snares.

Belonging to this or that religion,
Thinking that our group is 'right',
Is actually a trap of darkness,
Perhaps we're distracted by our own light.

But the light of others must be honored,
There are angels in our midst,
But we might be too busy defending our position,
Or chasing external bliss.

What we see in our brother,
Or what we really don't see,
Might have to do with our own suffering,
Through our ideologies we are not free.

The energy of many angels,
Visit this earth for the good,
They come clothed in many forms,
In Divine presence they have stood.

That person that we callously judge,
That person we decided to shun,
Because we thought we were holier than thou,
Was truly the holy one.

But so many don't recognize it,
With their noses so far up in the air,
Thinking they are saved and behave like an ass,
Because they dwell in darkness's lair.

Janine Palmer (Silver Moon)

Wounded Light

The love in his heart called her to him,
Even though his heart was wounded so deep,
The light he was still able to share with her,
Was a blessing she would always keep.

The woundedness still buried in him,
Would seep out to cut her down,
But it wouldn't erase the effects produced,
That he had brought a smile to what was once a frown.

It's the wounds which people carry,
Which emerge to release their pain,
And those who are very close to them,
Might feel like they've been maimed.

When they emerge they're not pretty,
Remnants of ego's lower face,
Unhealed festering hidden wounds,
Trying to come out to the light of grace.

We might realize we can't force something,
We can't carry on our own what can't be dually maintained,
But we can still hold a space of love for someone,
In forgiveness in the absence of pain and blame.

The energy of forgiveness and acceptance,
Is rising above what ego would have us believe,
And this is a step onto the path of Ascension,
Where truth is regained and blessings are received.

We are all wounded on this plane,
In this place where we create heaven or hell,
And by our free will choice and agency,
We determine how often we remain in a cell.

We gather wisdom from things we learn,
From people, places and things,
With no attachment to any pain,
Which illusion always brings.

What a blessing to meet our higher self,
When life's tests have thrown us to the ground;
And what unexpected treasures there,
Are waiting to be found?

Even though he was wounded,
He still made her feel great love,
And then it was time to separate their paths,
No point in trying to force on the wrong glove.

She also learned to take a step back,
From something which seemed so mean and cruel,
To detach just enough to find peace and to stand in her power,
Because no one else's unreleased pain, would ever be her rule.

Janine Palmer (Silver Moon)

Perception's Roots

They reacted to what they thought was truth,
They reacted to information incomplete,
They went into judgment's lower realm,
Creating from falsehood and unnecessary grief.

By believing things which were not true,
And reacting to them in kind,
They were unfair to another person in error,
There are ways we don't know we are blind.

Falsehoods rule this planet,
From illusions we shift and create,
Through ignorance we dance around the truth,
To the fire of judgment though hate.

Until we reconnect with our true power,
The power of unconditional love now bared,
The beauty of giving the best of ourselves,
To kindness and forgiveness for healing shared.

Janine Palmer (Silver Moon)

Screaming Ego

Why does he need to belittle others?
Why does he focus on flaws?
Why does he focus on the faults of others?
Of self-destructiveness why is he the cause?

Why does he put others down?
To build himself up, of course,
It's a nasty habit of the ego,
When from our higher self we are divorced.

Tedious, destructive little habits,
Patterns from programs and loops replayed,
And sadness, regret and depression,
Are frequent visitors to his days.

Because he hasn't taken his power back,
And because he doesn't know how,
Because he is chained to ego's cave,
Where he does not live in the now.

Trying to control other people,
Thinking that only his way is right,
While he sits bound in his dark cave,
Not able to reach the light.

Out of balance with so many things,
But not open to see or hear,
Because of insecurities and old wounds,
And self-doubt, resentment and fear.

Unreleased demons which plague him,
In the form of repetitive thoughts,
Because his own magnificence and divine love,
Is a thing he apparently forgot.

The screaming Ego is so loud,
He can't hear his own Sacred Heart,
All he wants to do is be loved,
But he chases them away with his darts.

If he could give himself great love,
And forgiveness of self and others,
He could begin to feel the connection again,
Between his sisters and his brothers.

Janine Palmer (Silver Moon)

The Suffering & Shadow

Karmic Challenges

What karmic challenges do we face?
Most of us do not know,
We don't remember what we came here for,
To balance and nurture our flow.

The suffering we experience here,
Is likely due to suffering we caused,
Because of something called cause and effect,
And because of Spiritual Laws.

We are given free will choice here,
By choice and consequence do we learn,
So things we experience here good or bad,
Are the result of the choices and actions we earn.

Dark and light and duality,
And the balance in between,
Rising above illusion,
When the truth in us is seen.

To remember our magnificence,
No being is unworthy here,
We know when we are ascending,
When we reach out to dry, rather than cause a tear.

When we witness the horrible effects,
Of extreme hatred from a being,
We can be sure there are unhealed wounds there,
Buried which we are not seeing.

From the ground on our knees, feeling all is lost,
From life's hardships, where we learn the most,
From the place where we surrender in acceptance,
Is when we release the ghosts.

Janine Palmer (Silver Moon)

Less Elegant

There are things in life less elegant,
In this earth school life like hell,
But there is beauty woven in between,
Singing from the angels and screaming from the wells.

There are things which test us greatly,
When they throw us to the ground,
And while we lay there in the dirt,
There is treasure to be found.

Elegance is a fleeting thing,
It's floats in but doesn't stay,
It comes and goes like storms of emotion,
Through dark and light and gray.

Elegance will flicker in to tease you,
It will bless you with a kiss,
And them something less elegant will follow it,
To steal away your bliss.

Because we are always tested,
And we are harmed by other's pain,
But there is always wisdom woven in between,
Which we will always gain.

Janine Palmer (Silver Moon)

The Shadow Side

I have had good friends,
With whom I assumed I could be myself in full,
I thought they accepted me as I am,
But by illusion I was fooled.

They might eventually try to control you,
They might eventually try to shut you down,
And so what was once a pleasant smile,
Transforms into an unpleasant frown.

Those who didn't accept me,
Those who pushed me away,
Actually pushed me to new parts of myself,
I was surprised to discover along the way.

I apologize for my mistakes and shortcomings,
In whatever way I should now,
Even though they know I meant no harm,
What if to illusion we no longer bow?

I apologize for misunderstandings,
I apologize for unintended oversights,
But now I must cut the cords,
With those who wish to fight.

We cannot be without boundaries,
Even with those we love and trust,
Because at some point misperception will rear its head,
And what was well nurtured will turn to rust.

Similarly we shouldn't have too many boundaries,
We can't function well with too many walls,
We must find a happy medium in balance,
Or we will continue to fall.

The shadow side of some people,
Might be more than we can take,
I mean the darkness of their unhealed wounds,
Which haven't seen the light un-faced.

The wounds which fester when buried,
In hidden places in the shadows not faced,
And when they try to come out,
They come in the form of anger, jealousy and hate.

When from them you feel unkindness,
Which feels like misplaced hate,
And for their unhealed business,
It's you they will berate.

This is when we must observe,
The issues which are not ours,
There is a cell they have created,
We need not stand behind those bars.

Don't get drawn into the prisons of others,
We must always find the gate,
To disconnect from any hell perceived,
And walk away from hate.

So thankful for neighbors upon this plane,
Who look out for those in need,
Who help heal and staunch the wounds,
Those of this world have caused to bleed.

But through the process of bleeding,
And through the process of the fire,
We strengthen or discard areas of weakness,
These are the blessings which transpire.

So you see there are many things,
Disguised as things which are bad,
But they redirect us to new things,
Which we needed but did not have.

It's so important to find the blessings,
From the terrible things we receive,
To sift the wheat from the chaff,
To release what would make us grieve.

Janine Palmer (Silver Moon)

Corrections & Alignments

As we navigate this crooked trail,
Of light and dark we walk,
As we learn to communicate,
From different perspectives as we talk.

As we learn to hold space,
For others and ourselves,
We find new pathways toward the light,
Out of the shadows where we dwell.

Sometimes the shadows serve us,
And sometimes we need the light,
We do our best to find balance,
Through the illusions of wrong and right.

Corrections and alignments,
Are needed to maintain,
To help us stay on course through the lessons,
Through the victory and defeat of the games.

We don't really lose anything,
By any experience we gain,
We have to look beyond the veil,
For divine truth unrestrained.

Janine Palmer (Silver Moon)

Disgraceful

When we dishonor our brethren,
When we are unkind here on this earth,
We hamper the grace of our journey,
The ascending path of our rebirth.

When we dishonor our brethren,
We do so dishonor ourselves,
Because the hell we might put others through,
Is a hell we create with ourselves.

Will you be a pillar of beautiful light?
Will you extend a hand to lift a friend?
Or will you find fault or a weak point?
Then attack them in egoic ignorance to trend?

Disgraceful can come from our old pain,
Our unhealed wounds which fester inside,
As the toxins try in some way to be released,
Where we buried them like they somehow had died.

No part of your temple is a tomb,
Not a place for painful things to be buried,
There comes a time to set your sack of burdens down,
They are weights which shouldn't be carried.

Old wounds which go on suffering within us,
Can explode to harm others in unfair ways,
So important to face the pain and release it,
Which will clear away so much illusion and haze.

Janine Palmer (Silver Moon)

Lessons

The lessons she was learning,
Where like initiations sent from hell,
Like trudging through the tar pits,
While the town's folk ring the bell.

The one(s) who came to help them,
The one(s) they burn or crucify,
The one(s) they always disbelieve,
Because they believe the lies.

While darkness wails and cries here,
There are beings which do feed,
Off of the fear and pain of the people,
The unhealed darkness which does bleed.

The venom oozing out of us,
While the dark lords sit and laugh,
Pitting brother against brother,
In our hands they place the gaff.

But we must remember our power,
We must take our power back,
Because the true color of our beloved hearts,
Is neither gray nor black.

The tar they throw which strikes us,
The stones they throw which break,
The pain they cause in our hearts and souls,
Are free tickets to hell's gate.

The stones they throw may pave the way,
That we may build a fortress strong,
When we use them to create good from bad,
As we rise above duality's song.

We create hell for ourselves here,
And we often create it for others as well,
Until we learn to release and let go,
Of the stories we like to tell.

The stories we hold are only perspectives,
And they are not complete,
There are parts we are yet unaware of,
Which can become a thief of our true peace.

When we longer feel the driving need,
To tell the stories which we need to release,
Or when we can tell them with no attachment or pain,
Then we have risen above our old pain and grief.

Grief is a silent killer,
Release it to the light,
So you can come back into right alignment,
With your love and truth and might.

Janine Palmer (Silver Moon)

Wicked

The wickedness of this earthly plane,
The ugliness hiding in this world,
Creeps out of the anger and pain of wounds,
Which when triggered are then unfurled.

Launched out like some lethal thing,
Belched forth from the bowls of hell,
Released from beings we think we know,
But obviously not too well.

Not well enough to prepare for,
The wrath which might spill forth,
The unhealed wounds which fester within,
Blocking them from their course.

Triggers, the ghastly triggers,
Causing the monster to come out,
Trying to inflict as much pain as possible,
Because within them they scream and shout.

Until one day when they unload,
The venom festering there in such hate,
And out it spews all over you,
From the bowls of some hellish gate.

Hold it not against them though,
Because that would be a trap,
Be in forgiveness because it's not about you,
How they are tortured to hell and back.

Self-torture because they lack the tools,
Forgiveness is the key,
But through the pain and illusion,
They cannot clearly see.

Hopefully one day they can effectively unload,
The wicked burdens they carry,
To heavenly realms to be transmuted,
Or to be purified in the earth if buried.

Bury it not inside thyself,
Thy sacred temple is not a grave,
Clear out what no longer serves thee,
To make room for the love ye crave.

Janine Palmer (Silver Moon)

Wounded Healers

Every being on this planet,
Experiences some wounds along their path,
At some level we must learn to heal them,
To separate the wheat from the chaff.

When we have learned the tools,
Which have assisted us to rise,
It's part of shedding old skins,
And moving past disguise.

We can be of help to others,
When we have done the work for ourselves,
But only when they ask us,
It's up to each person to step out of hell.

There are things we learn here,
In places of hell on earth,
We learn to rise above our own ashes,
To the beauty of our own rebirth.

In the shadows treasures are hidden,
In the desert were things still grow,
In the fires which burn and transform,
Leaving embers and coals which glow.

Even the wounded healers,
Still have wounds which remind them to rise,
But they are still very much able,
To help others see with new eyes.

New perspectives and tools for releasing,
For moving beyond the old to the new,
Taking the wisdom gained here,
As we heal new blessings come through.

Janine Palmer (Silver Moon)

Twisted

Some are masters at twisting things,
To get out of taking responsibility for what they create,
They like to twist things around and away from themselves,
Flinging it back at someone and slamming the gate.

The gate they slam is to their own prison,
Their own issues they deflect out of fear,
Because the issues of their unhealed wounds,
Are something they don't want to face or hear.

So they become like a ninja master,
And they twist things around so unfair,
Trying to pretend it's someone else's issue,
And that is the coward's lair.

Not taking any responsibility,
For the dysfunction they create,
Then they create more by shirking responsibility,
They create distance, detachment and hate.

They neglect themselves and others,
Hiding behind so many masks,
The suffering is extensive and ongoing,
As they continue to create more lack.

Don't twist your toxic creations around,
And fire them at the ones you love,
You can't hide forever from what needs to be healed,
It's time to take off the gloves.

Janine Palmer (Silver Moon)

By Degrees

By degrees we inch toward enlightenment,
By degrees we make our way back home,
By degrees we rejoice or suffer,
By our decisions along our path as we roam.

By degrees we remember the love we are,
By degrees we begin to ascend,
By degrees we cut the ties which bind,
Through the gate where ignorance ends.

Along the path of ignorance to knowing,
The path through the soul's dark night,
The path through the shadows of the forest,
To the magnificence of the meadow of light.

By degrees we begin to remember,
Our magnificence which comes from God,
And upon ourselves and our brethren,
No longer do we trod.

No longer do we doubt in fear,
No longer from our truth do we hide,
When we step into the light of divine love,
Where we came from and always abide.

Janine Palmer (Silver Moon)

The healed

When we help another to heal,
Any dysfunctional part of themselves,
It's because we have walked that road,
And learned it's no place to dwell.

We can't help them until they ask us,
But when we're ready to heal and to rise,
It's because we have important work to do here,
For the collective benefit of the tribe.

To help heal is to empower,
When we allow ourselves to heal we become strong,
Because we rise above a murky swamp,
Of a place where we don't belong.

Sometimes we feel we're drowning here,
This place is a dark testing ground,
But in the darkness are many treasures,
Just waiting to be found.

When we allow ourselves to be healed,
When we reach out to heal another,
We become more unified in the collective,
Through the thinning veil of separation, we begin to see our brothers.

Janine Palmer (Silver Moon)

Unaware

Sometimes there are aspects of ourselves,
Of which we are very unaware,
Good or bad traits, characteristics or habits,
We don't even realize are there.

Sometimes others see beauty in us,
Which we fail to see in ourselves,
Especially if we struggle with worthiness issues,
When we haven't yet come out of the cave where we dwell.

Sometimes we are so busy struggling here,
To do what we think is right,
So distracted by illusions and challenges,
We seem very unaware of our own light.

Then sometimes someone will point out,
The beauty they find in our being,
And then we are offered a glimpse of ourselves,
From a perspective we simply weren't seeing.

Similarly though due to our shadow side,
There are traits which might hamper our path,
Things like weakness, ego and unhealed wounds,
Which keep us in a place of lack.

Others might see it and point it out,
In ways we don't want to hear,
But it's when we can be open to what needs healing,
That our path will become more clear.

We learn from the light and the shadow,
We learn when we can more clearly see,
And others act as mirrors for that purpose,
To find the balance we need to be free.

Janine Palmer (Silver Moon)

Shadows of Ghosts

Hints whisper through creation,
Reminders of what was lost,
Not lost, but not remembered,
And lack of recognition is the cost.

But souls do you remember each other,
Glimpses of sparks as they fly,
Whispers of the faintest memories,
When they were you and I.

Dark shadows of ignorance dancing,
They knock and hide out of sight,
Only to emerge to trip us flat,
When something beautiful is in sight.

And the words which sometimes roll,
Off our lips and out of our bleeding hearts,
Things written down or whispered,
Are the remnants of divinity's sparks.

In this zone of free will agency,
Where we are free to create,
Here we create heaven or hell,
And forget we are the key to the gate.

Shadows of ghosts always linger,
In and around our space,
Challenging us to remember our divinity,
Because we are made of love and grace.

Janine Palmer (Silver Moon)

hell Bent

Over and over I see it,
The effects their wounds represent,
Like a monster someone let out of its cage,
On destruction it is hell-bent.

I've seen it unleashed on the innocent,
Looking for anything to hook onto,
To suck the energy from a person,
To twist and bend it unrecognizable.

Looking for victims like targets,
Someone to spew their venom upon,
Creating drama and strife for another,
To distract them from their own issues, so wrong.

The pain they inflict upon others,
Reflects the unhealed pain they feel inside,
And when they can no longer live with themselves,
The good in them is overtaken by the parts which died.

Not knowing how to help themselves,
Sometimes they reach out and sometimes they don't,
And beware if they ask and you help them,
They might turn on you so next time you won't.

Sometimes we can help them,
But we must have boundaries and barriers in place,
Otherwise they might disrupt,
The energy of our grace.

Until they release their demons,
The monstrous entities their thoughts did create,
Until they can enter forgiveness,
They will reside in behind Hell's gate.

Janine Palmer (Silver Moon)

The Dark

At first I was unaware of it,
The darkness which dwelled in him,
I only saw the light,
And his engaging, magnetic grin.

I knew that there was pain there,
I knew I was sent to help heal,
But only to a degree can we help heal another,
And then to karma we must kneel.

Their suffering might be their karma,
Things which they create,
We cannot interfere with what is written,
Or we enter suffering's gate.

The dark in him I could not heal,
It was up to him to let it go,
And finally I had to pull away,
Because his negativity was dimming my glow.

The oppressive energy hanging there,
Which affected me wasn't mine,
Sometimes we have to detach from the ones we love,
Or wither on the vine.

Darkness is a testing ground,
Darkness is ignorance in action here,
Darkness might make you feel like a victim,
Until that energy you clear.

We always need to tidy up,
To sweep dust and cobwebs away,
Or else we exist between barriers,
Which need not block our way.

We all have light and shadow,
Without balance, which will rule?
When we cut the puppet strings,
We no longer play the fool.

When we cut the cords,
To old pain and unhealed wounds,
That's when we take our power back,
And not a moment too soon.

I honor myself for walking away,
From what didn't serve my path,
I honor myself for disconnecting,
From the energy of another's pain and wrath.

From deepest compassion I hold space,
From that compassion I hold love very great,
But I will not exist or wallow in,
Dark energy of unhealed wounds and hate.

Janine Palmer (Silver Moon)

Illusion and the Veil

Make Believe

The way we react to illusion,
The way we react to information which is incomplete,
The way we feel pain which was never intended,
And in suffering we take a seat.

We imagine all sorts of injustice,
From our perception which is limited at best,
And so we walk around attached to illusion's pain,
Are we passing or failing the test?

We make believe someone meant to hurt us,
We make believe we didn't hurt someone else,
And when we do we forge the keys,
Which will fit the doors of our self-made cells.

When jealousy overtakes us,
And we allow it to lead us along,
We are not in our higher power,
And we might be dancing to darkness's song.

Darkness here represents lack of knowledge,
Like fear under ego's control,
When we're far from standing in our power,
When we don't hear the call of our soul.

Our soul is the light of divinity,
Our soul like an ember or spark,
Will we fan it with God's infinite love?
Or let it flicker in and out of the dark?

Janine Palmer (Silver Moon)

Twice Born

What does it mean to be twice born?
Are we talking about body or soul?
Bodies here are born and die,
But the soul continues to glow.

So much of earth life is illusion,
Misperceptions and confusion the norm,
While we climb the mountain of consciousness,
Through tough initiations to be reborn.

To be reborn here from the ignorance,
After our birth into the physical world,
Where we grow up with programming and conditioning,
The whispers of our truth barely heard.

We experience a type of rebirth,
After tests and trials on this lower plane,
We rise out of our own ashes,
When our inner truth is regained.

Different people experience rebirth here,
In many different ways,
There are many paths up the mountain,
And many ways out of the grave.

The graves can be ideologies,
The graves can be beliefs,
The graves can be chains to the ego,
Misperceptions and falsehoods the thieves.

To awaken is to be reborn,
To a higher dimensional level,
To rise above attachment to the physical,
Or thoughts about it which trap us like the devil.

Attachment causes suffering,
To learn to detach is to learn to be free,
To give yourself permission to remember,
The magnificence of you and me.

Janine Palmer (Silver Moon)

Destructive Entanglements

In this life we become so entangled,
In falsehoods, illusions and lies,
Trying to determine what is truth,
Learning to see past the disguise.

In life we become so entangled,
In emotion and pain unhealed,
Through traumatic life experiences,
And our peace it often steals.

We become entangled in feelings,
Of love and sometimes hate,
We must learn to release what does not serve,
To find the key to the next waiting gate.

Destructive entanglements are teachers,
They should not act as jail cells,
They are things we need to rise above,
To release ourselves from hell.

Stepping stones they should become,
When finally we cut ourselves free,
To reconnect with our own wisdom and truth,
Which is understood differently by you and me.

Janine Palmer (Silver Moon)

Priests of Unity

They are the Priests of Unity,
Because they have eyes to see,
Beyond the physical realm,
To the things which set us free.

Beyond the illusions all around,
Beyond the mists of the veil,
Beyond the falsehoods which keep man stuck,
Which cause him to wallow and wail.

Until he finds his power,
Which is connected to his truth within,
Which is something not found anywhere outside of himself,
That is part of the illusion, the sin.

The ideas man has of sin,
Things programmed in error by religions,
Which cause man to remain stuck in fear,
And it alters and affects his decisions.

The earth is a free will zone here,
By our choices and decisions we create,
But when we give our power away to false beliefs,
We hand our power over to more than just fate.

We have come here to be tested,
We have come here to rise above the lies,
But many of us can't seem to see more,
Than what is visible with our physical eyes.

The physical is only part of us,
The physical is the clothes we wear,
The spirit is the truth within us,
The brave will hear it when they dare.

The Priests of Unity for the collective,
They are guides like ghosts unseen,
Who whisper to us to remember our magnificence,
And to wake up from the dream.

The Priests of Unity are in us,
And what a glorious thing,
When we begin to awaken to it,
And we can hear the angels sing.

Janine Palmer (Silver Moon)

Illusion's Wings

Something nasty has been wiped away,
Something which no longer served,
Something which was obsessed with power and control,
Disrupting our radiant verve.

Some might call it an overlord,
Some might think it criminally insane,
Some might think it got away with horrible crimes,
But balance must be gained.

We must be aware at all times,
That we never have pure knowledge to judge,
Too often we act and react due to misinterpretations,
With partial and inaccurate information and then we won't budge.

We want to be right for our ego,
We want to defend our side,
But until we realize there is no separation,
On illusion's wings in ignorance we will glide.

When we stop hurting other people,
Is when we stop hurting ourselves,
That's when we begin to take our power back,
From the depths of our own hell.

Janine Palmer (Silver Moon)

Process of Empowerment

Your life by experience unfolding,
The process of trial and error,
All for the purpose of learning,
Learning how to free yourself from so many snares.

Snares of illusion and falsehood,
Things which claim to be right,
Shouting and preaching from soapboxes and pulpits,
Contributing to the soul's dark night.

But really they are clever tests,
To help you find your truth within,
To find your strength and power,
To rise above the illusion of sin.

Oh how they would love to keep you trapped,
For their lower god to feed off your fears,
The high God of the purest love,
Does not feed off of His/Her children's tears.

Be very aware my brethren,
That things are not quite what they seem,
You cannot get all your answers from a book,
Everyone interprets differently, their experience of the dream.

Misinterpretation and mis-translation run rampant,
Creating horrific errors and plight,
Creating separation between brothers and sisters,
And their egos of thinking that they are right.

The process of empowerment,
Is to come to know who you are,
Above and beyond what they tell you to be,
As you rise above earthly scars.

Janine Palmer (Silver Moon)

Illusion's Loom

Illusion's loom is a curious thing,
A force of confusion leading many astray,
A force of creation and destruction,
Of rebirth or of decay.

The result depends on the individual,
Who frees himself or herself from the grasp,
From the grasp of illusion's laughing folly,
When we slip off its crafty mask.

When we recognize an imposter,
When we break free of skins and shells,
When we walk out of illusion like a boss,
Is when we walk out of a man-made hell.

But illusion is also a teacher,
It's a nefarious testing ground,
But woven in between its clever web,
Are treasures to be found.

Pearls of such great wisdom,
Experiences by which we evolve,
Initiates of the Mystery,
As the wheel continues to revolve.

The loom we are ever weaving upon,
The tangled webs we weave,
Until we rise above illusions lair,
To which by fear we cleave.

Janine Palmer (Silver Moon)

The Power of Voice

For a while she could only whisper,
Because she hadn't yet found her strength,
Then through compassion and initiations,
From the fountain of her own truth she would drink.

The power of her voice here,
Allowed the power of her compassion to come through,
To remind anyone who would listen,
The answers you need are always found within you.

She answered to a deeper love,
Which she could not easily explain,
She shared it with the world,
For collective healing to be gained.

A force of love moved through her,
Through voice and word and deed,
For she was to help those who wanted it,
To heal the wounds which bleed.

Some would misunderstand her,
Some would so lash out,
Some would resist her whisper,
Thinking it was a shout.

But when she would shout they would listen,
Because the pain in her they recognized,
Was the same pain in themselves they'd been hiding,
Behind numerous masks and disguise.

Some grabbed hold of the light she offered,
And used it to heal themselves,
They were able now to become free,
From the darkness of illusion's well.

And so as a collective group,
We help each other to rise,
By the power of so many sacred voices,
Rising above the falsehoods and the lies.

Janine Palmer (Silver Moon)

The Mystery of the Heart

There is mystery all around us,
Between and beyond illusion's veil,
Within us in our complexity,
Beyond the crucifix and the nails.

The freedom from this lower plane,
By Ascension do we rise,
Each by our own free will agency,
Through different masks and dark disguise.

The heart holds many brilliant keys,
The heart is the spark of love divine,
The heart with the soul reconnected,
Is the path back to the tribe.

To rise above the self,
Or the identification with such,
Will serve us very well,
And bless us very much.

The self is the illusion,
The self might be the trap,
The whole learns when the self so suffers,
Until it takes its power back.

To take the power back from the lusting,
To take the power back into discipline,
To take the power back from fear and instinct,
Back to intuition as we all ascend.

But some of us are not ascending,
Some think they are not worthy thus,
Some are stuck in lower vibration,
In themselves there is no trust.

Those who become true seekers,
Those brave enough to find the truth within,
Can begin to disconnect from illusion,
And above the idea and trap of sin.

In the mystery is ever swirling,
So many hearts of the beautiful light,
Filled with wisdom and compassion,
Having risen above the soul's dark night.

Some are too identified with the self,
Whereby they dishonor others along their path,
Two enmeshed in physical matter,
That their own power they do lack.

To come to a place of acceptance,
Deep unconditional acceptance of the self,
To realize the self is the illusion,
We rise above to escape this hell.

Janine Palmer (Silver Moon)

Evil Does Not Rule It

Evil which comes from ignorance,
Is disconnection from God on high,
It rules nothing but illusion,
The fodder beneath the pyre.

It fuels such anger and hated,
For those trapped in such a state,
It feeds the bowels of hell on earth,
Which by fear and ignorance we create.

It doesn't rule the many,
It doesn't rule the light of the soul,
It might be part of the shadow which tests us,
As we progress toward the goal.

Evil does not rule,
Unless you allow it in,
It's an energy unhealed,
Which has nothing to do with sin.

It might come from missing the point,
And from the false ideologies to which we cling,
It might come if ego is our master,
It might come from the darkness we bring.

Until such time that we release it,
Release it to the flame,
Let it go without regret,
For the blessings we will gain.

Janine Palmer (Silver Moon)

Beyond Masks & Disguise

Honey or Venom

You attract more good with honey than venom,
Because nobody likes to be stung,
People don't really feel drawn to,
The venom dripping from your tongue.

Perhaps the love you might just lack,
Is the love you push away,
By your unconscious, protective reactions,
And the innocents you slay.

Maybe they started to like you,
Maybe what was started was a positive thing,
Until old habits and patterns took over,
And your buried shite you started to sling.

Maybe you harmed the very ones,
Who were on your path to help you heal,
But instead you lashed out from the pain in you,
And what was a good thing, your pain did steal.

How long will you allow the pain to rule?
When you carry a burden too heavy, set it down,
Dig a hole right were you leave it,
And bury it there in the ground.

Leave it there to be purified,
By so many forces here unseen,
Find the balance between light and dark,
To find the grace in between.

Janine Palmer (Silver Moon)

Dark Night

The dark night of the soul arrived,
From behind the mask of a friend,
Lashing out with poisonous venom,
To strike and strike again.

And it struck at weakened areas,
But that weakness turned to strength,
Where valuable lessons and stronger power,
Became an elixir I would drink.

Parts of me then died inside,
They were parts I did not need,
Like the serpent shedding its old skin,
And the wounds are cleansed which bleed.

Many arrows I pulled out that day,
From myself from another's hatred and pain,
A spear from my heart and healing commenced,
From the challenge came the gain.

From the festering pain of another,
Spewed upon me like the wrath of hell,
But woven in were positive things I found,
Through the tone of my soul's own bell.

And from the cruel treatment of another,
From their toxic venom so putrid and foul,
I found beneficial and rediscovered tools,
To rise above their tar pit now.

Rather than react in kind,
Launching a similar attack,
I recognized a tormented soul,
Screaming in pain and lack.

In forgiveness I must ever stand,
And in forgiveness I must remain,
To walk my path in grace and beauty,
And the dark night to restrain.

Janine Palmer (Silver Moon)

War Lords

Don't we all war with something?
At different points in life?
Until we learn to cut the cords,
Which don't serve us, with our knife.

We war with our own niggling thoughts,
We war with differing perspectives,
In defense of beliefs which might not be true,
Because control is our main objective.

Attachment to our ideas,
Attachment to our beliefs,
Attachment to wanting to be right,
Which can turn out to be a thief.

We war with the masks we've often worn,
We war with masks which others wear,
We might get offended, jealous or reactionary,
If and when we think others don't care.

When we think we have been disrespected,
We have a choice of how to react,
But reaction to misinformation,
Might come down upon us like an ax.

When we war it's always a choice,
Only we can decide if the choice is right,
But we should always carry the awareness,
That there will always be truth we lack from light.

So when you engage in battle,
With yourself or someone else,
Be prepared to learn something from the suffering,
Of your own or someone else's hell.

The hell here we all suffer from,
Is a nasty thing we each create,
And the fastest way to be free of it,
Is to disengage from hate.

Janine Palmer (Silver Moon)

Mighty Castle from the Stones

The fire burning in her heart and soul,
The fire of her ancient compassion,
The fire of love in her beautiful heart,
The fire of creative individual fashion.

The fire from the tears not cried,
The scars from the places they made her bleed,
The fire of truth burning within her,
Which contained all the strength and love she could need.

Some people can offer parts of love,
For limited periods of time,
But the love a being needs to sustain itself,
Is within them as it's connected to the vine.

People sometimes came along her path,
Who in some way she would recognize,
Soul mates of pre-agreements,
But they all have their individual disguise.

She came to recognize and cast off her own disguise,
To find her way to her truth of grace,
And in that place of compassion and acceptance,
Was the absence of any mask on her face.

The masks we have learned to wear,
To navigate this crooked maze,
When we struggle to see though illusion,
Through the initiations of this earthly maze.

The fire from the tears she cried,
Burned new paths for her to navigate,
And that included using as stepping stones,
The rocks they threw from hate.

And so those stones were gathered,
And a mighty castle was built from them,
And only warriors of divine truth,
Could find a way to get in.

Janine Palmer (Silver Moon)

Of Many Names Yet Nameless

We have been so many names,
But the names were just a mask,
Just part of the cloak and garment we wore,
To complete our earthly task.

The names we've experienced then and now,
Are only pieces of the Mystery,
And only when we shed them,
Do we then more fully see.

When too focused on the self,
We can't see what is beyond,
And therein lies the treasure,
The shackles are the bond.

We might respond to many names,
Once upon a time,
In different realms of experience,
Connected to the vine.

But it's our light which is our signature,
Names try to identify,
But names are only part of the truth,
The divine truth is you and I.

Janine Palmer (Silver Moon)

Declaration

He walked his path with purpose,
But that was not always the case,
For a time he stumbled in darkness,
By trial and error trying to find the right way.

The right way was the light of his soul,
The right way was his divinity recognized,
The right way led him to her,
And he recognized himself in her eyes.

She listened without judgment,
Her energy was a fair healing balm,
When he was with her his soul sang,
He felt love and blessed and calm.

He said, "I have a declaration to make,
We must walk our own path back to ourselves,
We won't find that full reconnection,
Until we walk out of self-made hell.

We do not find our worthiness,
Through acceptance by someone else,
What they reflect to us might show us,
What needs healing or to be cleared from our shelves.

I declare that I stand in gratitude,
For the blessings upon this earth,
The good ones and the bad ones,
Which steered me to my rebirth.

I stand in gratitude for the blessings,
Of the beautiful beings upon my path,
For the love and wisdom they share unconditionally,
And for how they make me laugh.

I thank the higher being(s),
Who I have discovered are my beloved guides,
And I thank myself for recognizing,
That behind any mask I no longer need to hide."

Janine Palmer (Silver Moon)

Attack of Trust

Being attacked by jealousies,
Disguised behind a mask of love,
Learning that trust is an illusion,
Behind the boxing gloves.

Trust is just and ideology,
About something for which we hope,
And on the other side of it,
Are parts of us dangling from some rope.

What we trust is always changing,
We are loyal to love because that's what we are,
When love stops being demonstrated and shared,
It created barriers, lack and scars.

During the flux of change,
In the absence of love people move on,
It doesn't mean they aren't loyal,
It doesn't mean trust is gone.

People must trust themselves,
They must be loyal to themselves when others are not,
They must honor the beauty of their own heart and soul,
When self-love might be something they forgot.

First we must be loyal to ourselves,
We should not expect anyone to make us happy here,
Trust issues come from unhealed wounds,
Heal your wounds and slay your fear.

Janine Palmer (Silver Moon)

Unless & Until

Unless and until you open,
To your potential to be free,
From limitations and illusions,
The purpose will continue to test thee.

Unless and until you remember your worthiness,
And stand in your power divine,
Free from the control of illusion,
You might stumble from time to time.

Unless and until you stand in self-love,
Where compassion is a nurturing well,
If you cling to old wounds or anger,
You will experience here self-made hell.

Unless and until you realize,
The lessons here help us to ascend and rise,
If you don't recognize the illusions thwarting you,
You won't recognize masks and disguise.

Behind the masks are bare truth,
Behind the masks innocence dwells,
Although it might be buried under layers of false belief,
It might be time to clear off the shelves.

Janine Palmer (Silver Moon)

Light Through the Cracks

The Path to Light

The path to the light is darkness,
The darkness reveals the light,
Sometimes we need to be where there is no light, to heal,
To let go of the illusion of control to tap into our might.

When we surrender the idea of control,
Due to ego and things don't want to face,
We can let go of fears to shed those skins,
With the help of divinity's grace.

Without what we learn from the darkness,
We wouldn't truly know the light,
It's above and beyond any conditioned ideas,
Of things labeled wrong or right.

It's all about experiences,
And what we learn about ourselves from them,
It's not about taking sides through duality,
It's about whether we share compassion with friends.

We must not think we are better,
Than anyone else on this plane,
We must not think we are holier than thou,
Religions and politics can make us so vain.

We must rise above ideologies,
Of thinking we are somehow right,
If we need to make someone else wrong,
We have already lost the fight.

The light dwells within the heart,
But it might only be an ember or a spark,
Which needs to be kindled by compassion and love,
Which is kindled in the dark.

Janine Palmer (Silver Moon)

Columns of Light

Maybe light needs dark to know itself,
Light reveals things in darkness unseen,
What we do here determines our course,
Lessons through experience is what we achieve.

Not just misinterpreted scripture's ideas,
Of what appears to be right and wrong,
But the truth which comes from our soul when it's free,
And how we share the treasure of our beautiful song.

Some of us are columns of light,
We leave columns of light where we stand,
We leave trails of sparking divinity,
As we do healing work with people and the land.

Some of us bring in darkness,
By way of our wounds unhealed,
For higher purpose unbeknownst to us,
For things to shift in illusion's field.

It's a two edged sword of mystery,
Buried anger begins to sprout,
Effecting others in what appears to be hurtful ways,
Through hell's door they scream and shout.

But the release of that pent up anger,
Shifting energies for reasons unseen,
Teaches us how to react or respond,
From the perspective of our dream.

When they hold up a mirror to us,
And we don't like something we're seeing,
We might argue and fight in resistance,
But through acceptance we connect with the truth of our being.

If or when they project something toward us,
And it doesn't trigger us in any way,
That's when we know it's not our issue,
We feel no need to react so in our power we stay.

The beauty and power of non-reaction,
Whereby your energy they cannot take,
Where the warrior stands in his or her truth and strength,
There is power in the choices we make.

Will you be a column of light?
Will you spew anger from the depths of your hell?
Will you learn what you can from every situation?
Then send love to fill your vessel, your well?

Janine Palmer (Silver Moon)

Encourage

I encourage you to love more,
I encourage you to disengage from hate,
I encourage you to be aware,
To everything you create there is a gate.

Would you be willing to walk through,
Anything on this earth you create?
What energy do you create from?
Is it love or is it hate?

I encourage you to love yourself,
I encourage you to live,
I encourage you to walk in kindness,
I encourage you to forgive.

I encourage you to forgive yourself,
Because you might need that gift from yourself,
I encourage you to use your key(s),
To release yourself from any hell.

I encourage you to walk in beauty,
I encourage you to stand up for what is right,
For whatever is right to you,
And be a warrior in your might.

Be not afraid to stand up for others,
As you would want them to do for you,
If it is ever needed,
To allow the love of God to come through.

Janine Palmer (Silver Moon)

Sunlight and Shadow

In the sunlight we might see more clearly,
But sometimes it's so blinding we can't see,
Sometimes in the shadows, balance we find,
The intensity of the sunlight sometimes blinds.

Sometimes in the shadows, if they are too dark,
When vision isn't clear enough, we might need light to spark,
Somewhere in the middle, is the balance which we seek,
Somewhere between humility and ego, exists the perfect meek.

The meek shall inherit, because of the balance they have found,
From passion and surrender, on their knees upon the ground,
The balance between opposing sides,
And rising above the illusions which lied.

Sometimes the sunlight and sometimes the shade,
The light in between is how we are made,
Turning the page and leaving behind,
The things which test us through life's constant grind.

Permission now granted from the truth of our Self,
Where wisdom and sacred love always will dwell,
When we rise above the illusions of this world,
That's when true beauty begins to unfurl.

Janine Palmer (Silver Moon)

Graves

The graves we carry within us,
From things we buried and did not face,
Created from the unhealed wounds we hide,
Because we are disconnected from our Grace.

The tombs of pain surrounded by walls,
And the bloody armor we create,
Then bury in places inside of us,
Which block our energetic gates.

There comes a time we must exhume,
The treasures from these graves,
To determine the value from things we learned,
And to change how we behave.

To change our repeating reactions,
Of perceived protection mode,
Which disrupts our balance and our verve,
Until the dogma we unload.

To dig deep into our internal graves,
And clear the cobwebs out,
So our being can feel free and clear,
For our happiness now to shout.

Dig up the inner graves of old,
And toss them into the fire,
The fires of transformative Grace,
To which it would be behoove us to aspire.

Janine Palmer (Silver Moon)

Wounded

The wounds are part of the experience,
The wounds are where the light comes through,
The wounds remind you of why you're alive,
The wounds are what connect me and you.

It's the wounds which tell the stories,
It's from the wounds we learn,
It's the wounds which strengthen our hearts,
As quietly we discern.

The wounded warriors are the strongest,
After they've taken the time to heal,
They are the ones who share their hearts the most,
Because they have nothing anyone can steal.

They give to the world all they have,
And slowly it starts to come back,
Because the more they seem to give,
The less they seem to lack.

The wounded healers are the most compassionate,
Because they had to learn to heal themselves first,
They had to learn to rise from their own ashes,
They had to learn through the process of rebirth.

The wounded have learned from the fires,
They have been through the fires of hell,
But they have come back to us now laughing,
And ringing divinity's bell.

They have learned a level of detachment,
Because others burned them at the stake,
Others threw venomous projectiles,
From deep, dark places of hate.

Others writhing is anger and pain,
Nailed them to the cross,
But they found a beautiful way,
To rise above the dross.

They are the survivors of this,
They're survivors of this spiritual war,
And they are the enlightened ones, my brethren,
Who can show you divinity's door.

Janine Palmer (Silver Moon)

The Broken Ones

Through the broken ones still standing,
And the broken ones on the floor,
When the light enters them through their cracks,
It will open so many new doors.

The broken ones who learn how to heal,
The broken ones who learn to forgive,
Are the strength of humanity who light the way,
For other broken ones in need of rebirth to live.

To take the treasures from the pain,
To take the knowledge they learned,
To take the strength they found in themselves,
From the transformative ash of the fires where they burned.

The broken ones who strengthened,
Weakened areas which held them back,
Who became their own pillars of balanced light,
Their own support for any perceived lack.

Things broken can be mended,
Or used as building blocks,
They can become the sacred keys,
Which open many locks.

Janine Palmer (Silver Moon)

Crack You Open

What if life cracked you open?
What do you think you would see?
What unneeded things would you release?
In cleansing yourself to be free?

What remnants of misunderstanding?
What unforgiveness is swirling around?
What sadness and what resentment?
And under that what would be found?

If and when you release the old anger,
You hold against yourself or anyone else,
There you would find the waiting door,
To free yourself from that hell.

And when the rubbish is cleared out,
What you find you just might not believe,
The beauty of your own light you buried,
Shining so brightly now that it's free.

The relief to you on so many levels,
The light there in your heart and your soul,
The feeling of connectedness to heaven and earth,
As above now so below.

Janine Palmer (Silver Moon)

Investments

Investments can be anything,
Anything worthwhile to you,
Something that when you give to it,
It gives you something back too.

Investing in relationships,
Investing in ourselves,
Investing in education in many ways,
To find our truth where wisdom dwells.

To find the truth within us,
Where sacred wisdom is stored,
Knowledge gained through experience,
Which opens many doors.

Investing in love and sharing it,
On the earth where we see great need,
And using it to help heal beings,
Whose hearts were left to bleed.

Investing in our souls,
As they are here to learn,
To remember our magnificence,
Through transformative fires which burn.

Invest in trust and faith,
Trust the path which is rocky sometimes,
Enjoy the views along the way,
Through this grand illusion of time.

Janine Palmer (Silver Moon)

Not Remembered

At different levels of spiritual evolvement,
At different levels of being open to learn,
At different levels of intuitive awareness,
The things we carry and the things we burn.

Even those who are more highly evolved,
Of a higher vibration and knowing connected,
There are still so many things not remembered,
Things hidden in shadow where light is not yet reflected.

So many things being remembered,
So much unfolding through Divinity's flower,
Yet so many things are still not remembered,
Between the stairs as we climb up the tower.

Magical things unremembered,
Hidden there just out of sight,
Yet glimpses of clues ever shine through,
Between the shadow and the light.

The battles which crack us open,
To discover hidden treasures in ourselves,
Because within us lives sacred divinity,
Unfathomable, the depth of our wells.

Janine Palmer (Silver Moon)

By Responsibility Untold

By responsibility so ignorantly shunned,
Twisted around and thrown at the one,
The one who shared with you their Sacred Heart,
At whom by old wounds you began to throw darts.

You can't seem to scale your own walls,
So relationships wither, suffer and fall,
And there you stand scratching your head,
Wondering why they end up dead.

Things not nurtured, but you don't see?
From responsibility for actions do you flee?
No matter how much they loved you, they couldn't seem to stay,
Because standing in your shadow, you don't see the light and the way.

Owning responsibility is being in power,
Not hiding behind the walls where you cower,
And so you begin to feel lonely and cold,
Feeling the victim because your story's untold.

Trying to make it to the fault of another,
Sets up your own fall while hurting your brother,
When you own what you do and own what you feel,
You stand in your power and by your decisions you heal.

Janine Palmer (Silver Moon)

Freedom Through Awakening

Collective

The pieces of you still with me,
The fragments of experiences we shared,
Parts of me on so many levels,
On the wings of the bravery we warriors dared.

Those moments throughout space and time,
In that temporary illusionary state,
Where we shared moments of love in full bloom,
Where we stood together at Creation's gate.

We share common memories,
A connection so strong it pulled us back together,
Sometimes feelings of wholeness so complete,
Sometimes floating away like a feather.

But because of our unhealed wounds,
Because of insecurities and fears which creep in,
Because of doubts and impatience,
Things slip away and that is the sin.

But this is also part of the learning,
This is all part of a higher plan,
To test our strength through the journey,
Of every woman and every man.

To learn to be able to walk away,
Without the love, but with the love still in your heart,
To detach from any resentment or pain,
Is where the beginning of our power really starts.

To be in gratitude for blessings,
Even when we think we are in lack,
Is to rise above the illusions,
To take our sacred power back.

There really is no lack, you see,
Only our ideas about such,
And when we truly love ourselves,
We will heal the collective so very much.

Janine Palmer (Silver Moon)

Collars

So many of us wear collars,
And the collars are attached to a lead,
But who or what is on the other end?
Does it nurture you or make you bleed?

Even if it doesn't make you bleed,
In any way that you know,
Does it cause you to mistreat a brother?
Does it stifle you or help you to grow?

Collars and leads to people and things,
Are similar to puppets on strings,
The wearer is controlled by some master,
And some masters are egoic beings.

A master can be anything,
An ideology, a culture, a church,
A person, an organization, or a fear,
Which interferes with any spiritual rebirth.

Take a closer look at who holds your leash,
Anyone or anything which wants you to adopt their belief,
Which may not be part of your inner truth,
And might turn out to be some kind of thief.

Those who follow along with group think,
Those who follow along blindly like sheep,
Thinking they're in the 'right' group,
Might judge their brothers because of belief.

Belief may or may not be truth,
No one can know but you,
No one can determine what your kingdom contains,
And taking off the collar will allow it to come through.

Janine Palmer (Silver Moon)

healed Ancestors

Some of our ancestors are healed,
Some of them have done the work,
Some of them have let go of old pain,
To embrace the rapture of their rebirth.

A rebirth of higher dimension,
Letting go of attachment to things,
To ideas or pain or hatred,
For the freedom that magnificence brings.

Ancestors cannot fully heal,
While clinging to earthly things,
Old ideas full of misperceptions,
Are the downfall of many dreams.

This earth is not where we come from,
This earth is a cosmic school,
The wise men of every tribe know this,
And detachment is one of their tools.

The respect we have for the elders,
Respect for the wisdom displayed,
In how they demonstrate to us,
That they are triggered not by darkness's games.

They who have risen above ego,
They who have mastered all things,
They who have passed the initiations,
And through ascension their healed hearts sing.

But there are ancestors waiting,
Who are still lost and connected to matter,
Who haven't yet mastered full wisdom,
To rise above all that mind chatter.

And when we hold onto their old pain,
We don't help them to let it all go,
We must learn to release so many things,
Which don't serve us or help us to grow.

We should not live in that place of old pain,
If we do then we cannot ascend,
We can't heal by keeping hated and pain alive,
In that negative energy the wounds will not mend.

Let us send love to the unhealed ancestors,
Invite them to let the pain go,
And when we learn to love all people here,
The Creator's light will begin to show.

Be a warrior for the ancestors,
Learn to share your love here,
Set an example of the wisdom and compassion,
Which frees all of us far or near.

Janine Palmer (Spirit Silver Moon)

Oh, Karma

Do you wonder about the suffering?
And wonder why it is 'allowed'?
Maybe you don't know about the concept,
Of karma from the fields you've plowed.

Cause and effect and balance,
To experience here what we create,
Suffering might be karma being balanced,
So we can move on now through life's next gate.

We don't mistreat any being here,
And walk away unscathed,
We are ever evolving here,
Through the grind of this earthly lathe.

Think twice before you lash out,
To harm another for any reason,
Even if it's from your unhealed wounds,
Because it's to your own spirit you commit such treason.

Janine Palmer (Silver Moon)

Waves

What comes to us in waves?
Whatever waves they are,
Waves of water, light or energy,
And the things carried in, which might leave scars.

Things which crash against us,
The waves bring in many treasures,
But differently do we perceive it,
In different perspectives and different measures.

Waves of many kinds,
Wash up treasures upon our shores,
Even if it only shakes up our lives,
To guide us toward new doors.

Do we run away from them?
Do we let them toss us around?
Do we allow them to wash over us to cleanse us?
Until their unknown treasures are found?

Do we listen to the sounds they create?
Some are silent and some are not,
Do we hear what they are trying to tell us?
Some things we remember and some we forgot.

Do they remind us of important things?
Do they bring blessings our way?
Do we remember to be in gratitude?
By the waves things are always reshaped.

Janine Palmer (Silver Moon)

Divine Solutions

Pieces of the puzzles,
Keys to the treasure box,
And wisdom is a master key,
To access sacred locks.

Wisdom floats all around us,
Some hidden, some in plain sight,
Some of it was instilled within us,
Found through our courage and might.

Solutions to many problems,
Created by illusions or not,
Solutions from the grace of divinity,
To forge and heal what was wrought.

To rise above so many labels,
To rise above misinterpretations,
Trying to please lower forces unknowingly,
By offering false libations.

The hounds howl in the distance,
Calling what to home?
The lost pieces of our hearts?
Which in confusion roam.

Pieces of our beloved souls,
Misplaced as they were by pain,
When we discover the key to our divinity,
We can call them back again.

Sovereign in our power,
But so many remember it not,
Apparently their worthiness,
Is something long forgotten.

Unworthiness programmed by so many religions,
Our worthiness comes from God,
But so much misinformation flying around,
Has it tied up in confusion's knot.

It's time to untangle the kinks,
Time to undo the knots,
By remembering our true divinity,
After descending here we forgot.

Not everyone is ready yet,
To let go of their old pain,
Because they don't remember,
What treasures they shall gain.

Divine solutions are contained,
As treasures tucked away in each being,
The magnificence of their kingdom within,
So many simply are not seeing.

When we become a true seeker,
Beyond ego is where truth ever reigns,
Where the purity and innocence of our souls,
Is nurtured and maintained.

Janine Palmer (Silver Moon)

Into Knowing, Beyond Belief

It's Called Wild Road

Was it the name of a catchy song?
Or was it the name of a story?
Was it about the destination or the journey?
Or was is about the guts or the glory?

The wild road for each being,
Is a different experience now,
And how they integrate and process the wisdom,
Is how to their truth they take a bow.

Is your truth something known to you?
Is it something you follow and think is real?
Or is it a deep and ancient knowing inside of you,
And is it connected to how you feel?

Is it wild when take a step forward,
Not knowing where the road leads?
Is it wild when the blood flows from fresh wounds,
Because of how our hearts sometimes bleed?

Is it wild when the mystery before you,
Begins to blossom and unfold?
When it reveals layers of hidden things,
The parts of the story heretofore untold.

The wild road is the vulnerability,
And in the vulnerability there is strength,
And when we are brave enough to share it,
Our warrior's colors we wave at length.

When we are courageous enough to share,
The parts of ourselves which are deep,
We gain treasures for the wild road,
Which are always ours to keep.

There are depths in all of us,
Which others often do not see,
And when we hide it away from the world,
We might be chained in fear, struggling to be free.

Those who walk the wild road,
Embrace the shadow and the light,
Those who embrace the Mystery,
Know it's about the experience and not about wrong or right.

Janine Palmer (Silver Moon)

honor the Spirits

There are spirits who honor us,
In ways we don't even know,
Some of us know and some of us don't,
Of other dimensions which are not shown.

Some of us honor the spirits,
And it's very well we do,
The ancestors who came before us,
And some still work through me and you.

Sometimes through our knowing,
Sometimes through things which inspire,
Sometimes through the call of our soul,
Toward important goals which transpire.

Some of us are sleeping,
Some are in denial and fear,
Some don't have the slightest clue,
What they are doing here.

To honor the spirits is respectful,
To honor them shows our grace,
To honor them honors the Father,
And demonstrates through truth our courage faced.

Janine Palmer (Silver Moon)

Sacred Power

The dark and the light exist,
By each other side by side,
Things we travel through and learn from,
Since we descended from on high.

Everything serves a purpose,
For reasons we haven't begun to comprehend,
Knowledge through experience is wisdom,
To our higher self these lessons we send.

What we learn as wisdom,
Becomes integrated as part of ourselves,
And we take our sacred power back,
Every time we walk out of hell.

Hell created here on earth,
By ignorant things we believe,
Which holds back and blocks our growth,
Of the ascension we are here to achieve.

So be very wary of belief systems,
Otherwise known as clever traps,
For how they take your sacred power,
Until you take it back.

Janine Palmer (Silver Moon)

In the (K)now

Something delivered at your feet,
A grueling and challenging test,
What appears to be a devastating blow,
Always an opportunity to do your best.

After it knocks you to your knees,
What will be your choice?
Will you look deep enough to learn something?
And allow it to add to the wisdom of your voice?

Will you find your strength in the midst of fear?
Will you find it in the midst of pain?
Will you find it among feelings of sadness?
And when you release them what will you gain?

Will the fear of the unknown unveil itself?
To be so much more than you thought?
When you somehow begin to understand,
There is so much more happening than you know or know not.

There are things for higher purpose,
There are things happening on other levels,
That are unfolding according to divine plan,
But we perceive them as frightening devils.

When we fall into a helpless victim role,
That is when we are powerless at our own feet,
And not much is usually gained,
When we take the path to retreat.

Although sometimes we might need to step away,
To regroup and to gather our druthers,
But from these tests we will ever learn,
What is the bigger picture here, sisters and brothers?

So when it seems that life is so unfair,
When it feels we have no power,
That is exactly the time we get to decide,
Whether to stay stuck in prison or bloom like a flower.

Remember, when you hold things against another,
When you hold things against anyone else,
You create for yourself a type of prison,
A type of self-created hell.

Give your worries to higher source,
Call in your angels when you're in need,
And be a gratitude for blessings known and unknown,
Because there are lessons to which we need to take heed.

Lessons which feel so devastating,
Often turn out to be blessings somehow,
But only for those with eyes and ears open,
Who find themselves present in the now.

Janine Palmer (Silver Moon)

Moving Beyond

Moving beyond the tethers,
Of programming from forces dark,
Darkness working through ignorance and fear,
Dimming the breath of Divinity's spark.

Moving beyond the fear and guilt,
Moving back into Love's full power,
Moving with the life stream of beauty,
Stepping for a moment out of illusion's hour.

Finding unexpected strength,
In the silence when we rest,
And then hearing our own familiar voice,
Guiding us back from initiation's tests.

Moving out of limiting belief,
Where false thoughts lead us astray,
Moving back into knowing,
Beyond the school of hours and days.

To walk once again with the Angels,
To find our hidden wings,
To honor Grace, ourselves and our brethren,
Is to hear the Divinity of God's love sing.

Janine Palmer (Silver Moon)

Metaphors & Deeper Truth

Agents of the Gods

Here for divine purpose so beautiful,
Here to bless and be blessed,
Here unbeknownst to many,
But who will see past the way they are dressed?

Only those in touch with their intuition,
Those who see with more than their physical eyes,
Can see past illusion and misperception,
Who can see the light shining behind their disguise.

Some can sense the pureness of their hearts,
Some can feel the pureness of their souls,
Some can see the light in their auras,
Shining divinely here now all aglow.

Some recognize them by their compassion,
Some recognize them by their grace,
Some don't know why they are drawn,
They just recognize something in their eyes or face.

They are messengers and they are teachers,
They are lanterns here on our path,
They are hope and love incarnate,
And they help us to take our power back.

They do God's work as warriors,
But compassion is their strongest tool,
Openness and deep understanding,
Help them crack open the shells of fools.

To crack them open to let the light in,
To open them to help them to heal here,
To help them rise above illusions,
To release anything now connected to fear.

Sacred Shamanic Whispers

To release what does not serve them,
To free them from their cells,
To show they the keys they hold,
To unlock any doors keeping them stuck in hell.

To hold space for those who are suffering,
To share healing and tools for such,
To let people know that they matter,
And that they are loved so very much.

And to remind them of the love they are,
To remind them their love is to share,
To reunite all Brethren to the collective vine,
By our thoughts and our deeds we are aware.

Janine Palmer (Silver Moon)

Weak Links

The weak link is where they target us,
So strengthen the places in need,
So that no one can use them to harm you,
They will have no power to make you bleed.

To be vulnerable and transparent,
Is a strength often not realized,
Unless there are still parts unhealed,
Hidden behind some disguise.

But when you've strengthened the weak parts,
By detaching and releasing them free,
There is no power they can take from you,
Because of bare truth and honesty.

When you own your truth and share it openly,
For the purpose of sharing wisdom gained,
Then they can't use it against you,
In your open honesty you stand unrestrained.

Janine Palmer (Silver Moon)

Appear to Face

The left hand receives,
And the right hand gives,
The mind it thinks,
And the heart it lives.

Thoughts create,
And thoughts destroy,
Do you hide?
Or do you deploy?

Do you take action?
Do you learn, then in forward motion go?
Do you get hung up in the feelings of pain?
Where the suffering feels like crawling through hell so slow?

Do you gather in your forces?
Do you discard what you don't need?
Like the old pain you carry around,
Which continues to make your heart bleed?

Do you know that grief is a process?
To feel the feelings and let them flow through,
Not something which should stay stuck in you,
Which can kill you if you don't allow room for things new.

Receive what comes, with dignity,
Stand or kneel in grace,
Release and give away old burdens,
To lessen the suffering you appear to face.

Janine Palmer (Silver Moon)

Not Intentional

I know it's not intentional,
The pain which you create,
Which comes from your unhealed wounds,
Of stored pain and anger creating such hate.

I know that you are reaching out,
On levels which you don't know,
The volcano has erupted in you,
Spewing forth the venom to restore your glow.

The people it's directed toward,
Need to take a step back and to the side,
To step away from your venomous projectiles,
And simply let them fly.

Not to allow them to get stuck anywhere,
Not to take anything at all personally,
To recognize there is more going on,
Than a person should take to be about 'me'.

Some people need to purge,
They know not how to heal,
And the nastiness which comes forth from them,
Their friendships they damage and steal.

People often push us away,
When that is not their conscious intention,
They're at a place where they don't like or accept themselves,
Which they are too ashamed to mention.

Hold space for those who are suffering,
Give them space and learn to detach,
Because they are in the midst of a rebirth,
And their healed version hasn't yet hatched.

Be an observer and a witness,
And from these events you shall always learn,
Learn to release what no longer serves,
Throw it in the fire to burn.

Janine Palmer (Silver Moon)

Darkness's host

Darkness might try to justify itself,
Because pain is such powerful fuel,
But that power depends on being fed through loops,
Its own destruction is its very best tool.

Not the dark that is part of us,
The dark which is lack of knowledge and unreleased pain,
The unhealed wounds of venom which fester,
To create doom and gloom and rippling shame.

The jealousies we tend to hold onto,
And how they will then eat away,
Until we finally lash out,
Harming others who stand in the way.

The people who care and try to help us,
The people just trying to walk their own path,
The people who are fighting their own battles,
And we strike them with our own gaff.

Maybe they trusted us enough to confide in us,
Maybe they shared what troubled them most,
And then there are people who would use that against them,
And then you have darkness's imbalanced host.

As they continue to self-destruct,
They will try to take others down too,
Unless and until they can heal,
They aren't able to let the light through.

Forgiveness would be essential,
But first they would have to forgive themselves,
For by holding things against others,
They are keeping themselves locked in their cells.

To stop finding fault in others,
Oh what a glorious key,
To look for the good in all we meet,
No unforgiveness, no jealousy and we're free.

Let us not hold others hostage,
Because we are doing it to ourselves,
Let us heal and mend the brokenness,
While together we walk out of hell.

Janine Palmer (Silver Moon)

Temperate

Temperatures of opposite extremes,
Hot and cold each they burn,
Opposite ends of the spectrum,
And between the two we learn.

Extreme heat can burn us always,
But extreme cold can burn us as well,
We need to find some middle ground,
Through illusion's cells as we walk through hell.

It's the warmth of grace and compassion,
Which flickers in our heart's well so deep,
That surfaces to be shared with others,
The treasure we share and we keep.

When we notice a being is hurting,
When we notice someone lost in the dark,
When we notice someone struggling is quicksand,
We act in care through God's own spark.

Not everybody will reach out,
But thank God for those who do,
The light of the Creator works through our brethren,
When certain beings allow it through.

There are some people we can help,
When they want it and they ask,
Some we can't help because they're not ready,
They are still learning through each task.

Some will be resistant,
Some will fling their venom about,
Some will suffer in silence,
And some will scream and shout.

Some will make up slanderous lies,
Or believe things which are not true,
So many suffer from believing illusions,
And it sticks to them like glue.

When we take a step back things,
And begin to realize,
That behavior comes from deep issues people carry,
Things which terrorize.

When we cease to react to the drama,
And stop allowing it to draw us in,
When we stop feeding the monster, taking our power back,
And peace wins over the supposed sin.

Janine Palmer (Silver Moon)

Witches' Wings

What if those they burned as witches,
Were really angels here?
Doing God's work as healers,
But those in darkness couldn't see their light through fear.

Clothed here in human guise,
Continuing to do holy work on earth,
Angels of the burning fire of love,
To help humanity with rebirth.

So many shun what they don't know,
They judge what they don't understand,
They label and hide in their boxes,
While all around them the shit hits the fan.

These loving angels of divine fire,
Reflect the goodness and holiness of God,
They were created from the purest love,
But upon them men do trod.

In their ignorance which is darkness,
Men try to control and rule,
But they are lost sheep gathering fear,
Which is spun from them like wool.

Angels here as heretics,
Trying to share deeper understanding of the divine,
Were hung or they were burned,
Your brothers and sisters and mine.

The fire the angels were created from,
Burns hotter than any fire of hell,
So be careful who you think you burn,
From behind your dogmatic cell.

Be not forgetful my brethren,
To entertain strangers unknown,
For thereby some have entertained angels,
Unaware of what they were being shown.

So many believe the twisted lies,
Served to us pretending to be light,
While darkness laughs at our suffering,
The angels help us through our plight.

Janine Palmer (Silver Moon)

Created and/or Creative

Created from the energy of Love,
Spirit undying so fair,
Changing form and appearance,
Light dancing in and out of thin air.

Descending into places,
Forgetting origins divine,
Lower vibrational energy,
The illusion of yours and mine.

Creating realities and experiences,
In this free will zone,
Spiritual laws like karma,
For what we create we must atone.

What will we create on our journey?
Will it be labeled as good or bad?
How will we treat our brethren?
Will they feel happy or sad?

Just a little reminder here,
You will have to experience what you create,
Be prepared to taste your creation,
Be aware whether you create from love or hate.

Janine Palmer (Silver Moon)

Blood Soaked Virgin

The virgin is the pureness of spirit,
The purity which is the soul,
No earthly journey can taint it,
The divinity of God's energy glows.

It shines brilliantly through beings here,
Through their magnificent love as light,
Vibrations dancing, drawing us in,
Unless we are distracted by wrong and right.

False ideologies programmed in us,
Things we were taught were wrong,
Rattling around like traps tripping us,
Stealing the breath of our song.

And so our lower self through ego,
Likes to point the finger in blame,
Likes to find fault so frequently in others,
Knocking them down in the falsehood of shame.

Creating suffering in others,
Creates so much suffering in ourselves,
And so would begin to create,
Our very own self-made hell.

And then we try to justify,
And then responsibility we want to take,
And then we might think we are superior to others,
Which creates the path now to Hell's gate.

Not recognizing the virgin,
Which has nothing to do with sexual acts,
Not recognizing the purity of the spirit,
In the sleepwalking collective in lack.

They would try to crucify the virgin,
If a virgin they think she is not,
But the blood dripping from the virgin,
Is the false ideologies they bought.

The blood from their misunderstandings,
The blood from the churches' lies,
The blood from forgetting their origins,
But the blood drawn from the disguise.

Janine Palmer (Silver Moon)

The Gods

They say many things here and there,
Throughout history in countries near and far,
They shout it from the pulpits,
And whisper behind doors ajar.

They each have their own perspective,
And 'they' of course includes 'we',
They say the gods believe in nothing,
For things above belief are free.

So out of touch are most of us,
So disconnected from the gods,
Evidence of this can be seen,
By how upon our brethren we trod.

How greed and lust and ignorance,
And ego, fear and strife,
Are the very things which cause our pain,
Until we cut the cords with our knife.

To cut away the anger,
To cut away unforgiveness too,
To bless each other with divine love,
Is how our Grace comes through.

Janine Palmer (Silver Moon)

Of 1000 Names Yet Nameless

Energy vast and creative,
Of knowing, love and light;
And mankind has tried to name it,
But none can get it right.

No human understanding,
Or words could comprehend,
An energy indescribable,
With no beginning and no end.

Man tries to make it in their image,
But in their image man was made,
The kingdom and the garden within,
Of Sacred things written on a page.

So many names through the illusion of time,
So lovingly here bestowed,
Upon the nameless so beloved,
As above, now so below.

Janine Palmer (Silver Moon)

Channel

Like channels of water which flow out,
From a greater source at higher levels afar,
Feeding other bodies for deeper purpose,
As are beings here, that's what we are.

We are channels here of divine love,
But along the way debris blocks our path,
You must continually work to remove it,
And in between the work we must laugh.

We channel best we are open to flow,
Often water has been likened to spirit,
It flows to those are open and receptive,
To those who are in gratitude now to hear it.

We channel for the greater good,
Through free flowing love from the source,
Unless there is too much built-up debris,
Which will restrict the flow, of course.

There are some who would build a dam,
To block the flow from on high,
Starving out others down the line,
Without nurturing from source we die.

What do you channel here freely?
What do you allow to flow?
Do you maintain your conduit frequently?
Which nurtures your soul's divine glow.

Be in gratitude for the channels here,
For the love and wisdom they share,
They are simply extensions of something greater,
All connected from here to there.

Janine Palmer (Silver Moon)

Perspectives & Treasures

The Secrets

The wind it told a story, every time it blew,
It whispered of things which came before,
It spoke about ancient wisdom woven in,
Through thoughts and hidden doors.

It spoke of so many tears,
And it spoke of so much pain,
But it also spoke of great love shared,
Which was a reminder of what we have to gain.

To recognize the glimmer of distant truth,
To vibrate at a higher vibration here,
To regain our connection to the love we are,
Which comes when we rise above fear.

The wind will remind us if we listen,
About how it brings in and blows out the clouds,
About how it blows away the dust which accumulates,
Sometimes it's a whisper and other times it is loud.

Sometimes it's cold and it freezes,
Sometimes it cools us in unbearable heat,
Sometime we embrace it laughing,
Sometimes we turn away and retreat.

The wind once told me about you,
It told me of your beautiful heart so battered,
It told me about how you often hide away,
From the world because you were shattered.

The wind told me of gruesome histories,
But the wind also told me so much about love,
It told me secrets of the mysteries,
As below and so above.

The wind told me about the trees,
And the healing to all they provide,
And the wind told me to take you there,
Because nothing from them will you be able to hide.

The wind said that you are ready,
To release the burdens you carry,
And that dancing in the shadows just out of site,
Is the enchanting presence of brave little faeries.

The wind said the faeries know important secrets,
Which they will share with the pure of heart,
The wind told me they have a gift for you,
It's a treasure map which will shows where to start.

They said you have to trust yourself,
And allow yourself now to smile,
Because the illusions you have experienced here to date,
Were only designed to beguile.

The wind said to tell you thank you,
For your bravery here on this plane,
And there is so much more going on behind the scenes,
Which can't be understood here or explained.

The wind said it will be explained later,
In another higher dimension,
Where we will be glad to visit again,
When we are done rising above hell's extension.

The wind is the breath of spirit,
The holy breath of the collective soul,
The breath of life mixed with fire,
Is what give our life its glow.

Janine Palmer (Silver Moon)

Doors

At some point she began to open,
To levels before unknown,
And the more open she became,
The more things were being shown.

To use the term unknown here,
Really means unremembered,
Until we peal back the limiting veil
To move beyond to what will be rendered.

So many intuitive beings,
Recognizing aspects of her soul in many facets,
Telling her things about who she had been,
Things she had never dreamed before this happened.

And when she began to open more,
To accept things which at first seemed strange,
When she felt humble and grateful for it,
Her perspectives were rearranged.

She began to recognize certain aspects,
Of so many parts of who she was,
And how they all tied into her calling,
With her raven and with her dove.

And in some of the doors were windows,
Showing glimpses of other things,
Deeper parts of the complexity,
But every one of them sings.

And the mists of the illusions,
Began to be cleared away,
And the light shining in was glorious,
From the truth, the light and the way.

Janine Palmer (Silver Moon)

Transition to Treasure

Through transitions like waves ever changing,
Sometimes fierce and sometimes weak,
The revelations to us of hidden things,
But first we must endeavor to seek.

Little pieces of a grand puzzle,
As hidden treasures begin to present,
Things hidden away by the force of the waves,
As we let go of resentment when we repent.

The meaning of repentance or metanoia,
Is to change one's perspective throughout the game,
Because what we come in as and how we leave,
Are not meant to be the same.

The treasures gained here are of love and pain,
Because of how they sharpen the blade,
And the pearls of wisdom we take with us,
Through the choices that we made.

The treasures we must search for,
And when we're ready we will find,
Which open us to our heart and soul,
And release us from the ties which bind.

Treasures not recognized by many,
But when you're ready they'll be recognized by you,
And when you are open in wonder,
You will allow them to come through.

Many are closed and don't know it,
Don't be closed off in belief,
Don't be too attached to certain ideas,
These hide the treasures, they are a thief.

Treasures are stored in places,
We don't even know exist,
And you shall only discover them,
When you no longer so resist.

Janine Palmer (Silver Moon)

home

What is home to you?
What things call to your heart?
Places you've been which speak to you,
Or something from which you can't be apart.

Is it a place your heart has been?
Not in this lifetime but you seem to know it so well,
Does it call to your heart and soul?
Like the tinkling sound of a bell?

Is home an indescribable connection?
Is it being near the ocean or among the trees?
Is home creating art which flows through you?
Does it feel like any of these?

Is home writing books or poetry?
Because they connect us to some other gate?
What if words could shift us now?
To a place of love from a place of hate?

Janine Palmer (Silver Moon)

Teacher and Student

Does the teacher become annoyed with the student,
When student begins to grow and flow?
Does the teacher become jealous in any way,
When the student flies off to places unknown?

Does the teacher sit in observation,
Even when he or she doesn't understand anymore,
What fuels the flight of the student,
To venture through unknown doors?

Is it possible that the student,
Might have a calling the teacher doesn't fully understand?
So then does that teacher try to hold the student back,
With sharps words and reprimands?

Is what the teacher thinks he sees,
They only thing really going on?
To point out things of importance is necessary,
But so is the student's response.

Is the teacher a temporary guide for the student,
Doing work here for higher reasons still unknown?
Is it possible there are things he or she doesn't know or need to know,
About where the student is going, by what they are shown?

Will the teacher be able to disconnect,
When it's time like a mother bird,
And allow the student to share their voice,
For things that are waiting to be heard?

Can the teacher sit in non-judgment?
Can the teacher allow it be?
Knowing he or she was an integral part,
Of something bigger they couldn't yet see?

If a student expresses thanks in genuine truth,
And if the student shared wisdom as well from their being,
Would that be enough of an exchange between them?
As things are created on levels we're not seeing.

Janine Palmer (Silver Moon)

Shock Therapy

Sometimes we just plod along,
Finding new things about which to stew,
So busy focusing on the negative,
We don't see new blessings coming through.

So busy holding onto hurt,
So busy holding onto old pain we carry,
That we don't release the sludge of it,
So it backs up and certain parts of us it buries.

And so then come the shocks of life,
Meant to roust us out of a place,
Out of the hell we've mired ourselves in,
Back to a more natural state of grace.

The things which shock our systems,
Designed for us to awaken,
But we often don't open recognize it as such,
Because our truth and wisdom we have forsaken.

Things which appear to be horrific,
And things we appear to lose,
Are all part of our learning journeys here,
Which comes about by the things that we choose.

Even if we don't at first see it,
Things happen for reasons we don't easily see,
For the purpose of sharpening the perspectives,
Of the intricate aspects of you and me.

Janine Palmer (Silver Moon)

hostages

Are you a delightful hostage?
To how some religion tells you to be?
Do you give your power away to perception?
Do you feel in any way here not free?

Does love flow freely from your heart?
Do you share with anyone in need?
Or do you feel separate, needing to prove others wrong?
Not caring whom your actions cause to bleed?

Are you a hostage to ideologies?
Are you hostage to misperception's noose?
Do you know that God is within you?
And your experiences come from what you choose?

Are you held hostage by any old pain?
Anything negative you haven't released?
Is anyone else in control of your path?
Have you conquered your own inner beast?

Some people let their beast out,
To maim others without regard,
Which places speed bumps along their karmic path,
Which will make them trip very hard.

When you stand in your own power,
Then you shall be a hostage no more,
When you take responsibility for your actions,
And allow your compassion to open new doors.

Being a hostage is when you allow anyone or anything,
To have any power or control over you here and now,
Until you find your inner truth and inner warrior,
And to no outside source do you bow.

Because heaven is within you,
Or any hell which your create,
God is in your heart,
You'll discover when you open that gate.

God is not outside of you,
Not only to be found through a church,
God is where we come from,
Whom we connect to through rebirth.

The ego can hold us hostage,
If we allow it to be in control,
It is only ever a servant,
Don't allow it to disrupt your flow.

Janine Palmer (Silver Moon)

Tidal

Things come in waves to test us,
Things flow in and things flow out,
Sometimes we struggle when the tide is high,
We try to tread water as we are thrashed about.

But when the tide gently recedes,
We often find treasures it washed in,
If we take the time to look for them,
In between the tides is where new perspectives begin.

The music of the ocean,
The music of the wind through the storms,
The music from our tattered sails,
Through life's experiences ripped and torn.

But there are always ways of mending,
Things broken, battered or harmed,
Which come from the love of the divine and through people,
Through the grail of light of the heart.

Janine Palmer (Silver Moon)

Rejection

Is it really rejection?
Is it rejection of us or them?
When we feel rejected in any way,
Could it be from wounds that just won't mend?

When someone seems to reject us,
It might be because they cannot be present for themselves,
We don't know what battles a person fights within,
Maybe they are existing in some quiet type of hell.

If someone or something is directed away from you,
It is for a deeper reason yet unknown,
Be patient for the reason to reveal itself,
In divine timing it will be shown.

Don't assume it's about you,
Although maybe there is something in you which needs to heal,
Because if something is meant to be yours,
It will be something no one else can steal.

Sometimes things and people here,
Are only meant to be temporary in our lives,
Even though it feels like it hurts to lose them,
And it feels like we've been cut with knives.

We must learn to change our perspectives,
Acceptance and surrender are powerful tools,
That is the beginning or taking our power back,
So we do not suffer fools.

Rejection has many faces,
Most are illusion's snares,
Be willing to look behind the curtain,
Blessings come to those who dare.

Janine Palmer (Silver Moon)

Limited Perspective

Seen only from one angle,
Not from 360 degrees,
It's only a fraction of the whole,
And we react to these.

With limited information,
Only seeing a fraction of the pie,
And we think we know all it contains,
So we then believe a lie.

To take partial information,
Standing in front of a lock without a key,
Is what it's like to judge a fraction,
Ignorance if you please.

Reacting without pure knowledge,
In the position of judge and jury,
Creating pain and suffering from reaction,
Because ego is in a hurry.

Quick to drop the gavel,
Quick to judge what we know not,
Too quick to solve a problem,
Because compassion we forgot.

Janine Palmer (Silver Moon)

New Doors

I learned the hard way about boundaries,
We must be careful who we think we can trust,
Because people have hidden and buried issues,
And when they present they can hurt you so much.

Misperceptions are vile heathens,
They are thieves of happiness so sad,
They will use things they have twisted against you,
Making you wish boundaries were a thing which you had.

They will use things against you in foul ways,
Due to their issues they've buried inside,
Due to unhealed wounds they sabotage,
What they once loved until the connection has died.

They destroy connections which once were bright,
They dishonor their very best friend,
And in loneliness and self-loathing,
They stay distant and refuse to bend.

A disgusting display of humanity,
Like an unexpected venomous attack,
Wounding and maiming God's beautiful creatures,
And they don't know how to take it back.

They don't seem to know how to correct it,
Due to a debilitating thing called pride,
They can't seem to rise to or above the occasion,
To bring new life to what they attacked which died.

The key is when we learn to let go,
Of something which was so special before,
So we can learn and gain from new blessings,
As we walk boldly through new doors.

As we walk forward in beauty,
As we walk forward in grace,
We do so with boundaries for our protection,
So others will respect our space.

Janine Palmer (Silver Moon)

Falling Out

Most of us have experienced a falling out,
With a person whom we love(d) so deep,
Because what we experience always changes,
The wisdom and memories are what we keep.

Situations and people change,
Perspectives of things change too,
Due to illusion it's always incomplete,
What we think we know, affects what we do.

So many of us act or react in error,
To the limited information we receive,
And so we do damage to kind people,
And cause them to suffer and grieve.

It's up to each person to determine,
What they learned from anyone or anything,
To learn to release suffering and grief,
And to find new reasons to sing.

Janine Palmer (Silver Moon)

The Colors of Love

The colors of love are ever-changing,
Blending and flowing as they vibrate,
As they are fed and fanned in energy,
Which we focus on or create.

The beauty we share or withhold,
The magnetic brilliance when recognized,
Of the fathomless depths of the mystery,
Of a being through the color of their eyes.

The colors of love through the words we speak,
Through the passion flowing forth from our soul,
From the language of the sacred heart,
As divinity there overflows.

That love is a powerful elixir,
It nurtures unspoken parts of ourselves,
And when we believe the illusion we've lost it,
When we perceive a falsehood of hell.

The love we come from and the love we are,
And the love we so create,
Can never really be lost to us,
Though we might lose sight of the gate.

When we cease to honor it,
We might not see it so clearly anymore,
And so it might remain hidden,
Behind some mysterious door.

Honor the Love here always,
Even the love you think you lost,
You don't lose what you create,
But misperception might be the cost.

The cost for not honoring Love here,
Might be a misperception of a thing,
And when we believe any falsehood,
At some point it will sting.

Janine Palmer (Silver Moon)

Lay Down Your Arms

Lay down your weary sword,
And I will lay down mine,
Where is the illusive peace?
We are supposed to find?

I often find it in myself,
And I sometimes find it in you,
Until the monsters scream for release,
While our emotions boil and brew.

I've noticed so many want to label me,
But that I must reject,
The misperceptions of others,
Are part of both of our tests.

Limited perceptions are tricky,
Like a room full of angled mirrors,
Which one reflects something perfectly?
None of them, my dears.

What you see in anyone,
Is only a very small part,
And if you attack what you don't understand,
You might dim the glow of your own spark.

Do you know the root cause?
Of the behavior you might see?
No, likely you only see the tip of the iceberg,
And in ignorance you are not free.

While the swords are on the ground,
Where they can harm God's children not,
Let's heal with love all the wounds we can,
Form the remedies we forgot.

Let us not say unkind words,
Let us not nail innocents to the wall,
Let us not dig our own graves,
Where we might just trip and fall.

When I share my heart with you,
Treat it with respect,
Don't use me as a dart board,
For your own healing you neglect.

I shall no longer tolerate,
The negative energy you hurl my way,
Take responsibility for the poison you puke,
It's your friends your venom slays.

Janine Palmer (Silver Moon)

Depth Perception

What do we really perceive,
From any limited perception?
Not seeing 360 degrees,
Not seeing the whole reflection.

Only really seeing a fraction,
Only part of a mysterious whole,
And so we react to incomplete knowledge,
Stuck in the valley below.

Do we really see the infinite depths,
Of any being along our path?
No, we only see by limited perception,
Because knowledge is what we lack.

Be ever aware of the unseen,
Be aware of the unknown in any case,
Beware of what is hidden,
Behind the mask on every face.

Old wounds which aren't yet showing,
Old pain buried in some tomb,
Things experienced making people behave in certain ways,
As they are weaving life through illusion's loom.

The bits and pieces of information,
Which you lack about a thing,
Might make you react in error,
And yourself or another will sting.

Be open to the glaring fact,
Of how we all suffer upon this earth,
And everyone is at different levels of rising,
To the event of their rebirth.

Janine Palmer (Silver Moon)

Building Philosophies

What treasures here are locked away?
What remnants of broken memories?
Who then are these fallen ones?
Who travel valleys and jagged peaks.

We travel the broken pathways,
Sometimes here we feel buried alive,
Missing steps and stumbling,
Forgetting our connection to the tribe.

Knowing not that sacred truths,
Have so been stripped away,
So stepping stones we must place,
As we evolve and make our way.

We all build our philosophies,
Sifting through empty promises sold,
Everyone here has been betrayed,
Until our truth in love unfolds.

Perfect impostors in beautiful masks,
Pretending they aren't fenced in,
Trudging through the swamps and mists,
With a few tears and an occasional grin.

Apostasy can mean divine freedom,
Depending on the initiate unfolding,
When they find God is within themselves,
Not in some preacher's false scolding.

As a being so re-discovers,
The consciousness of the Christ all around,
No longer need he suffer from false control,
Because the fear they sell is a foreign, offensive sound.

The love of God we share with our brethren,
Is the only sacred truth divine,
It is something that is part of us,
Who are connected to the vine.

Janine Palmer (Silver Moon)

The Lion's Map

He began to learn more about ego,
From a mere wisp of a girl,
Because she had begun to learn about her ego,
And a new map began to unfurl.

He taught her different perspectives,
She showed him entrances to once secret doors,
They became teachers and sacred confidants,
As they traveled from shore to shore.

He showed her deeper parts of herself,
Things he could see which she could not,
She helped him to open to deeper parts of himself,
To discover ancient wisdom long forgotten.

They each helped the other to unfold,
Many fascinating treasure maps,
And behind the door of each initiation,
Were restored parts and pieces they lacked.

What they thought they lacked was always there,
But initially hidden from them in some way,
And so the recognition of each other's souls,
Was reuniting with a love which always stays.

As they each raised their individual vibrations,
They held space in honor for the other,
Because any love shared unconditionally,
Is the greatest gift to a sister or brother.

The Lion is the ego,
Which will guide you to certain things,
Things to be learned, accepted and risen above,
And to the lion we should not cling.

Janine Palmer (Silver Moon)

You Become What You Hunt

You become the thing your search for,
What you search for is searching for you,
But doubt and fear and shame,
Will not let it through.

You become what you create,
You become what you consume,
It is always a good idea,
To sweep away the old with your broom.

Feed the love within your soul,
Listen closely to your heart,
Because the wisdom hidden silently there,
From you is never apart.

Search for the truth within you,
Search not outside of thyself,
The treasure of life you hunt for,
In stored within yourself.

Janine Palmer (Silver Moon)

The Leather Pouch

He carried a small leather bag,
And in it were treasures unknown,
In it were magical items,
And to no one were they shown.

A medicine bag hung around his neck,
In it important things were retained,
Things of meaning beyond material wealth,
And for love he would maintain.

He carried an ancient arrowhead,
From a flaming arrow which once flew,
Into the love of the heart of an ancestor,
The ancestor of me and you.

In the pouch he kept a lock of hair,
The hair from a noble horse's mane,
A horse which rode into battle,
Faithfully time and again.

The pouch contained a feather,
Of the raven's secret of creation,
Containing magic and wisdom.
Of the key to liberation.

In the pouch he carried three seeds,
From special ancient trees,
And when he found a sacred place,
By magical waters, he would plant these.

Each of the three items in the pouch,
Would be planted with each seed,
To be purified in the womb of earth,
To purge, to grow, to bleed.

Keepers of the keys and gates,
Upon this earth they walk,
Shape shifters here unrecognized,
For treasures to unlock.

The sacred and the holy,
Is the love in any thing,
To honor love in any case,
Is to rise above and sing.

Sin is the unknowing,
The unremembered state,
Not remembering our magnificence,
And so suffering we create.

But love the mighty power,
Will transmute any type of pain,
Love thyself first and foremost,
Lack comes from restraint.

Janine Palmer (Silver Moon)

Stories, Guides & Whispers of Love

Kingdom of Compassion & the Company of Horses

The hart stood at the top of the mountain,
Looking down at the kingdom there,
Looking over the realm of the princess,
He was a guardian for her so fair.

The hart was a mighty stag,
The keeper of wisdom's might,
To guide and protect her valiantly,
Morning, noon and night.

He kept near to her in the castle,
He kept near to her in the keep,
He kept an eye in her continued happiness,
He sent comfort when she would weep.

The angels sent the hart to her,
He was an angel there in disguise,
Because she had an important duty here,
She was sent to stop their cries.

She was sent to them by the faeries,
She was a special being here now,
She was of grace from the Tuatha,
To no one would she bow.

She ruled the kingdom with compassion,
She ruled from a place in her heart of grace,
She was quiet, regal and charming,
She carried a sword and dressed in lace.

She was a warrior but most didn't know it,
They didn't know what was behind her cloak,
They didn't know the burden she carried,
With no one to share the yoke.

She walked in mysterious beauty,
Watched over so by the stag,
Angels and faeries were all around her,
And she carried her very own flag.

She saw beauty in every being,
She saw beauty in everything,
She existed in a state of gratitude,
To the trees she loved to sing.

She kept the company of horses,
She loved their gentle spirits so kind,
She spoke to them in gentle whispers,
And they spoke to her in kind.

The animals were her advisors,
She could hear their spirits speak,
The trees offered her their guidance,
And comfort when she would seek.

The blessings of her castle,
Were the blessings love so gave,
And the power of the princess,
Was that she was honest, true and brave.

Janine Palmer (Silver Moon)

The Dragon's Seeds

A dragon protected her sacred lair,
To help her with the work she must do,
She would go to the woods for treasure and guidance,
She was open to allow wisdom to come through.

One day she found a treasure acorns,
On the ground beneath her favourite tree,
An ancient and mighty oak,
Who shared guidance because she believed.

She spoke to the trees and she listened,
And they guided her true on her course,
Along with so many other beautiful guides,
Along with many spirits of the horse.

Magical creatures would show up,
When needed along her path,
Archangels and Ascended Masters,
All she needed to do was to ask.

Spirit guides and animal guides,
With valuable wisdom to share,
From parallel times for the greater good,
When she called they were always there.

She gathered up some of the acorns,
From that very sacred place,
And she took them home and scattered them,
Nurtured by the light of her grace.

And the dragon would protect them,
To make sure they would germinate and grow,
Because the seeds held the wisdom of the mysteries,
And in anchoring heaven and earth they would glow.

The dragon was a force of magical strength,
Of protection from realms on high,
Assisting God's children doing their work,
As they walk the fine line between dark and light.

Janine Palmer (Silver Moon)

Sleeping Dragon

The dragon slept for a period of time,
Waiting for her to awaken,
It was only a matter of divine timing,
Because her calling would not be forsaken.

When she began to step out with curiosity,
Of the dogmatic box she was in,
The dragon was called to action to assist her,
To peel away layers for her journey to begin.

He started with the wild fires,
To burn her house to the ground,
Because there were treasures in those ashes,
Which were meant now to be found.

Under the pile of ashes,
She would eventually find a new road,
But she would have to shed and overcome burdens,
It was time to lighten the load.

She would have to learn detachment,
To step away from any perceived pain,
She would learn to rise like the phoenix,
For what she was meant to gain.

She would discover her calling,
Important things she was meant to do,
Not the first time she'd been called here,
It was time again to bring healing messages through.

It was time to be a voice for certain people,
Because they were ready to awaken to hear,
We share what we learn from our stories,
But we must rise above the stories to see clear.

The dragon was happy with her progress,
And he eventually made himself known,
Through the process of unfoldment,
When she was ready to be shown.

And what a mighty force he was,
Now that she was happily aware,
To have his presence so near to her,
To know that such a being did care.

One of her many helpers,
One of her many beloved guides,
One of the many to help her ascend,
Beyond the illusion and the guise.

Janine Palmer (Silver Moon)

Mermaid Song

On a meditative shamanic journey,
She was led to a precarious ledge,
At the edge of a great volcano,
Where a spirit animal guide nudged her over the edge.

To burn away the old shells,
To experience a shamanic death,
In order to be rebirthed for moving forward,
She had to pass these challenging tests.

And when the old was burned away,
A trap-door then opened up beneath,
Dropping her into a pool of healing water,
For transformation to bequeath.

Dolphins were there to meet her,
Shark and orca were present too,
Dolphin took her to a rocky ledge,
For transformation to come through.

The mermaids came and sang to her,
They sang directly to her soul,
To remind her who she was for her calling,
They were there to restore her glow.

Healing for the parts which had been mistreated,
She had been harmed and knocked to the ground,
But she always to be found something down there,
Treasures were always waiting to be found.

There were things which she had conquered,
There were ways in which she had to rise,
Tests and initiations to face the fear and pain,
And to shed any old disguise.

It all had to do with illusion,
And realizing what wasn't real,
Learning to recognize misperceptions,
To trust the truth we feel.

Janine Palmer (Silver Moon)

Say Yes

An Angel visited her in her dreams,
With a message about saying yes,
Because there are certain things when we allow,
Open us to new places very blessed.

Say yes to being observant,
In the absence of judgment's fire,
For what you will learn for knowledge,
While unseen blessings transpire.

Say yes to offering love to others,
Even in little ways,
Because feeling love upon this plane,
Helps us move forward through the haze.

Say yes to receiving divine love,
Because love you so deserve,
And as you do, it will nurture your heart,
And your soul's bright radiant verve.

Say yes to quiet reflection,
To ponder what you learned from a thing,
In gratitude take the wisdom,
Release what doesn't serve, to let your heart sing.

So yes to all types of forgiveness,
Because forgiveness is what sets you free,
Forgiveness of self and others,
Rising above the little me.

Say yes to self-respect,
And yes to respecting your brother,
In realization that there is no separation,
It serves no purpose to fight against others.

Say yes to releasing old anger,
Anger can be used as fuel,
For positive forward movement,
To rise above illusion's dark duel.

So yes to releasing grief and sadness,
To process it and release,
So it doesn't become a roadblock,
Or a debilitating quiet thief.

Janine Palmer (Silver Moon)

A Scabbard with No Sword

He traversed from village to village,
He shared positive news of light,
He wore a scabbard without a sword,
He'd decided there was no need to fight.

Once upon a time a brave soldier,
But nothing did it avail,
A sword against a brother,
Does not allow one to prevail.

He laid down his sword one morning,
He offered it to the Lady of the Lake,
He said upon this earth he would no longer need it,
And it was for humanity's sake.

The Lady said she would hold it,
She would keep it safely away,
No longer now would this warrior,
For any purpose endeavor to slay.

She said she would help him find balance,
Only with love and only with words,
But they both knew that only a few people,
Were ready for the truth to be heard.

So he would walk his ministry,
Sharing wisdom with those evolved enough to ascend,
Those who were open enough to listen,
Who wanted nothing more than for suffering to end.

He would walk with no weapon,
Because no one needed protection from love,
And his constant companions, besides visions of the Lady,
Were the raven and the dove.

Janine Palmer (Silver Moon)

Spinning

The sage met an interesting creature,
She was a complex entity, he would often say,
He could see many aspects of her being,
From the past, the future and today.

He had a vision of her spinning,
Once upon a time,
A high priestess of a sacred order,
Here to nurture the vine.

But what was it she was spinning?
What creative force did she weave?
What was her purpose and her power?
And what did it achieve?

What did she spin into this reality,
Form higher dimensions than this?
What wisdom and love did she weave in,
Of the fire and love of divinity's bliss?

What was the ancient twinkle,
Of knowing he saw in her eyes?
What was this depth of compassion in her,
Which she could never disguise?

What was the space within her heart,
That was waiting for a particular love?
And why did she always have the sacred company,
Of the raven and the dove?

What was the sword she had hidden,
Because its power was now too much?
Only one could wield it,
But the time had passed for such.

How come when they came to her,
Some of them weren't very kind?
When others were her truest friends,
Reconnected on the vine.

Janine Palmer (Silver Moon)

Airborne

The dragon circled airborne,
Above the village in the valley below,
Assigned as guide and protector,
To a goddess who didn't know.

He watched her vigilantly from afar,
Observing and intervening when he saw a need,
And compassion from his heart ever flowed,
As he quietly watched her beautiful heart continue to bleed.

In her free will prison here,
She must continue to learn by choice,
Through the wretched pain of initiation,
She must find and use her powerful voice.

By leaps and bounds she was rising,
But unseen chains had still held her back,
And the nefarious illusions swirling here,
Which presented themselves as lack.

The sleeping fools surrounding her,
Buried quite deep in their pain,
Hampered by their unhealed wounds,
Continued to strike and maim.

Those ruled by sleeping ignorance,
Who danced on puppet strings,
Who didn't recognize her goodness,
And the darts they threw would sting.

Those people who should share their love,
Would only demonstrate neglect,
Thoughtless and selfish actions,
Creating feelings of non-acceptance.

Rejection toward the kindness she offered,
Kicked when she was down,
Pierced her heart and left it bleeding,
But something special was happening in their town.

Before a burning fire of intention,
On her knees in surrender and release,
The dragon could see emerging from her back,
The power and brilliance of her wings.

Upon her grueling journey,
Upon the earth school plane,
Through a gauntlet of initiations,
Her warrior goddess would sustain.

A higher level of goddess revealed,
There from her now did emerge,
With an explosion of divine light glowing,
When all her old pain and negativity was purged.

And so the dragon chuckled,
In happiness and admiration,
Because he beloved little spitfire goddess,
For her love and grace and higher vibrational manifestation.

She had overcome her own demons,
She had found her kingdom within,
She rediscovered her magnificence and power,
The next level now would begin.

One day she would be able to see him,
Her dragon protector guide,
Even though she sensed his presence,
For now his visibility he would continue to hide.

Janine Palmer (Silver Moon)

It Was the Dragon

It was the dragon for divine purpose,
An instrument for higher purpose here unseen,
To help me step out of my earthly disguise,
So my heart and soul could sing.

The fire from the Dragon,
Helped disconnect me from preoccupation with material things,
For me to step out of my earthly self,
To begin to catch glimpses of my wings.

To burn away through wildfire,
Things I thought were important to me,
To clear a new path toward my calling,
Which before I could not see.

Under the guise of loss was redirection,
A new path began to unfold,
It was dark and light and shadow,
It was silver and white and gold.

All the colors filtered in,
Of the divine rays and angels and guides,
To lift me to a higher mirror,
For my higher self to recognize.

I learned much more about angels,
And things I couldn't see here,
I learned to let go of conditioning,
And falsehoods, lies and fears.

I experienced unkind treatment,
From those I thought were my friends,
Until I learned the ignorance they swim in,
Was darkness's unhealed wounds which needed to mend.

I learned about forgiveness,
About healing the heart and soul,
Spiritual and emotional healing,
Which brightened my soul's glow.

I heard God's angels reminding me,
I heard the Ascended Master guides,
I learned to speak directly to,
The beautiful light of Christ.

I began to become reacquainted,
With the gift of angels wings,
And they worked through me with the light of the word,
To share messages of love with many beings.

Janine Palmer (Silver Moon)

Satchel

He carried a magical bundle,
A leather bag strapped to his back,
And in it were tools of grace,
Which helped him to take his power back.

Sometimes he would reach in for wisdom,
Sometimes for patience and grace,
Sometimes for deep faith when needed,
When he was tested by the human race.

There were things in the satchel which helped him,
To remember these resources within,
Sometimes he would forget and stumble,
But he had the tools to begin again.

In there were reminders of self-love,
In there was light for the path,
In there was the sword of divinity's might,
To cut away any anger or wrath.

And in there was a quiet dagger,
A knife to cut unforgiveness away,
To cut the cords with what no longer serves,
Tools for falsehoods to slay.

In the sack was a cloak for secrecy,
A representation of the great Mystery,
And also in there was a lantern bright,
To shine on all he needed to see.

In his satchel was a single red rose,
To remind him of her love so fair,
To connect with her he just had to go into his heart,
To find her waiting there.

Janine Palmer (Silver Moon)

Seeds of Intention

The clouds came rolling in that day,
Oh the rain they did greatly need,
It would also begin to nourish,
Her newly planted seeds.

She had planted the seeds of intention,
Blessed with sacred breath,
To call in love in abundance,
Another initiation and another test.

To allow herself to receive what would nourish,
Because she was worthy in every way,
Because of the pureness of her heart and soul,
Because she finally accepted herself one day.

She would no longer hold things against herself,
Illusions they were anyway,
She would no longer hold things against anyone else,
Or her own happiness she would slay.

The storm swept him in on a gray horse,
Tired and drenched to the bone,
She invited him in for dry clothes and hot food,
Now her horse in the barn was no longer alone.

The rain was nourishing her intentions,
The universe delivered to her through a great storm,
And so a connection of sacred grace,
Was nurtured before it was born.

He had also set an intention,
Which he had scattered to the wind,
A similar intention and the universe answered,
Which was delivered now, as it was time to mend.

The wind is the spirit in motion,
The rain is a nurturing force,
The fire was the burning between their hearts,
While the trees anchored heaven and earth of course.

Janine Palmer (Silver Moon)

Found

He discovered a woman lying there,
Peacefully by a stream,
He wondered if he should disturb her,
She seemed peacefully in a dream.

When he approached, her eyes opened,
She stared at him for a while,
She didn't look curious or frightened,
But neither did she smile.

As he began to read her energy,
He could see she'd been hurt many times,
He could see the wounds and weapons there still,
He could even see the tears she'd cried.

He could sense an icy coldness,
A protective barrier she'd put in place,
And he didn't miss the twinkle of hope,
Which flickered across her face.

Gently he did lift her,
And carried her to some place safe,
And as he did he felt a tear,
Escape now down his face.

Visions flashed before him,
Of how they'd mistreated her,
All he wanted to do was to heal her,
Of those memories which were a blur.

She herself was a healer,
But she didn't have sufficient boundaries around,
So those in pain and anger,
Threw their daggers, knocking her to the ground.

He removed a spear and a dagger,
From her energetic space,
He sent her healing light,
And he began to see her grace.

He sent love to her deepest wounds,
And he watched her while she slept,
In prayer he called in angels to heal her,
While silently he wept.

His tears of compassion helped to clear away,
The remnants of darkness's wrath,
To heal the wounds to this kind soul,
Where they had hooked her with their gaff.

The cruelty of this world,
Had almost torn her down,
Until he happened across her path,
To chase away her frown.

As she began to mend,
In body, mind and soul,
In emotions, attitude and insight,
Her light began to glow.

He taught her how to smile again,
He reminded her how to play,
He taught her how to release from herself,
Any energy dark or gray.

He showed her that this world,
Contains many beings of love divine,
And God will send them to you,
At precisely the right time.

At first you might not recognize,
Just who they really are,
But they are beings of light like you,
Who originated from the stars.

She learned to be in gratitude,
And daily did she pray,
For the blessings here bestowed upon her,
From the truth, the light and the way.

Janine Palmer (Silver Moon)

halo

Her halo was glowing so dimly,
That he wasn't sure if it was there,
Light usually surrounded her like the stars,
She was a radiant angel so fair.

Sometimes her halo was brilliant,
Like happiness and love all around,
From the vibrations of somewhere higher than this,
Although most couldn't hear the sound.

But she gave so much to others,
That they drained her light sometimes,
She was a vessel of light needing refilling,
For her work for the collective vine.

He swept her away with him,
And led her off to the trees,
Where she could listen to birds,
And the leaves dancing on the breeze.

He took her to a babbling brook,
To dip her feet there in,
And he began to see her light come back,
Along with an engaging grin.

Grounding her in nature,
With the help of the ancient trees,
The best medicine here one earth,
Along with pure love if you please.

He held her softly in his arms,
Sharing the energy of love,
And for the briefest second,
He could see her wings as white as the dove.

Janine Palmer (Silver Moon)

About the Author

Janine Palmer (Spirit Silver Moon) grew up in Northern California and resides in San Diego today. After devastating county-wide wild fires in Southern California and global economic collapse, Janine and her family endured physical, economical and emotional losses, along with the loss of friendships. Judgmental treatment by so-called religious people (family/friends) caused her to question religions due to poor treatment by others in religious ideology. These initiations tested her inner strength and caused her to investigate more deeply for truth, what brings true happiness, forward movement, the evolvement of the soul and ultimately she discovered her calling.

She was a phoenix who rose from her own ashes with a powerful story to share of truth, strength, wisdom, compassion, love and taking one's power back. We must remember our magnificence to in order to rise above so much illusion. Looking for answers, Janine Palmer (Silver Moon) extensively studied and continues to study multiple healing modalities for emotional and spiritual healing.

Janine has studied World Religions, Spirituality, Early Christianity, Gnosticism, Philosophy, Critical Thinking, Biblical Scholars, and Spiritual teachers. Janine is a Clinical Hypnotherapist and Shamanic Practitioner. In the spiritual and emotional arenas, Janine has studied and become certified in the following areas: Cognitive Behavioral Hypnotherapy, Ericksonian Hypnosis, Energy Psychology, Emotional Freedom Technique (EFT or Tapping), Kinesiology, Muscle Testing, Neuro-linguistic Programming (NLP) the language of the mind, and

Reiki Master. She is also trained in Gamma Healing for overcoming energy vampires, healing emotional traumas, anxiety, depression and PTSD, and Shamanic Journey Work.

These modalities are helpful for releasing stress, old pain, resentment, anger, doubt, grief, unforgiveness or anything which blocks forward movement. Through her healing sessions, whether held in person, via phone or skype, she has helped others heal, grow, overcome obstacles and move forward lighter after releasing what no longer serves. This knowledge and wisdom is contained within her writings of uplifting messages for healing. She shares tools we can use to assist ourselves and others on their path. Janine is the author of multiple books containing many genres and messages from various teachings and modalities. The four main genres are story poems, romance, rising above dogma and emotional and spiritual healing. These are presented as poetic tales which have received very positive support and feedback around the world.

Janine's compassion and calling to help others break free of limiting and painful situations can be felt through the writings contained her he book series Divine Heretic. She does God's work for humanity, for the collective and greater good. It is a gift and a blessing she is very grateful for.

www.ingramcontent.com/pod-product-compliance
Lightning Source LLC
Chambersburg PA
CBHW071258110526
44591CB00010B/708